MW01235613

Fred Flatten has been a part of my life and ministry for many years. It was my joy and my challenge to see his faith fulfilled and walk with him into Pastoral Ministry. Those days were not always easy but a decision was made to accept the challenges and to continue in the walk of obedience to God's Call.

The walk of faith is not a cake walk. Pastoral ministry has its challenges: preaching, teaching, leading, challenging, confronting, and leading a congregation into steady growth and the walk of faith. Being a leader of the People of God is not without its struggles. What do you say when the news headline tells of a giant leader in evangelical ministry being exposed in gross immorality. Who can you trust? Who can you follow? Is it possible to succeed in living the "Christ Life"? A saying often heard among a rough, tough group of motorcyclists is right: "*Don't just talk the talk. Walk the walk!*" Rev. Fred takes us on that journey.

It has been my joy to follow Rev. Fred through the maze to an excellent ministry. He leads us all the way. There is a rest for the people of God, but no stopping place. Rev. Fred doesn't miss a turn. We are *In it for Life.*

—Rev. Benjamin Drown

Rev. Fred Flatten's words lead us to another level of understanding. His explanations and summaries were refreshingly clear and pretty entertaining as well! His style is unique and enlightening. The way that Rev. Fred Flatten has laid out his points are such that they "stick with you" which is so important when exploring God's word - the read is time well spent. Rev. Fred Flatten provided us with the "meat and potatoes of the stew" and he even explained some of the "petals of the onion in the stew" by revealing layers of topics that previously left us scratching our heads. It's a must have on our journey to be fruitful servants.

—Brian and Diana Gourley, Henderson, MD

in it for LIFE

in it for LIFE

A Spiritual Roadmap on the Quest for Discipleship

REV. ALFRED FLATTEN

TATE PUBLISHING & *Enterprises*

In It for Life

Published by Tate Publishing & Enterprises, LLC
127 E. Trade Center Terrace | Mustang, Oklahoma 73064 USA
1.888.361.9473 | www.tatepublishing.com

Tate Publishing is committed to excellence in the publishing industry. The company reflects the philosophy established by the founders, based on Psalm 68:11,
"The Lord gave the word and great was the company of those who published it."

Cover design by Amber Gulilat
Interior design by Jeff Fisher
Images by Amy Flatten

Published in the United States of America

ISBN: 978-1-61566-604-1
1. Religion, Christian Life, Spiritual Growth
2. Religion, Christian Life, General
09.12.30

DEDICATION

Dedicated to my loving wife Judy;
Forty-three years ago I said, "I do," and I knew,
I was in it for life!

Twenty-seven years ago, I said the same words
to Jesus Christ, and again, I knew,
I was in it for life!

TABLE OF CONTENTS

Become: The Wondrous Story of John 3:16

Believe: Getting the First Buttonhole Right!

Grow: Getting to Know God Better

Mature: Where Do I Grow from Here?

Be-loved: This Is My Command

Be Filled: the Spirit-Filled Life

Living Life from the Overflow: Blessed to Be a Blessing

Conclusion:

Become: LIFE

THE WONDROUS STORY OF JOHN 3:16

Introduction:

A STORY OF NICK AT NIGHT

"Now there was a man of the Pharisees named Nicodemus, a member of the Jewish ruling council. He came to Jesus at night and said, "Rabbi, we know you are a teacher who has come from God. For no one could perform the miraculous signs you are doing if God were not with Him." In reply Jesus declared, "I tell you the truth, no one can see the kingdom of God unless he is born again." "How can a man be born when he is old?" Nicodemus asked. "Surely he cannot enter a second time into his mother's womb to be born!" Jesus answered, "I tell you the truth, no one can enter the kingdom of God unless he is born of water and the Spirit. Flesh gives birth to flesh, but the Spirit gives birth to spirit. You should not be surprised at my saying, 'You must be born again.' The wind blows wherever it pleases. You hear its sound, but you cannot tell where it comes from or where it is going. So it is with everyone born of the Spirit." "How can this be?" Nicodemus asked.

"You are Israel's teacher," said Jesus, "and do you not understand these things? I tell you the truth, we speak of what we know, and we testify to what we have seen, but still you people do not accept our testimony. I have spoken to you of earthly things and you do not believe; how then will you believe if I speak of heavenly things? No one has ever gone into heaven except the one who came from heaven—the Son of Man. Just as Moses lifted up the snake in the desert, so the Son of Man must be lifted up, that everyone who believes in Him may have eternal life. For God so loved the world that He gave his one and only Son, that whoever believes in Him shall not perish but have eternal life. For God did not send His Son into the world to condemn the world, but to save the world through Him."

John 3:1–17 (NIV)

"For you know that it was not with perishable things such as silver or gold that you were redeemed from the empty way of life handed down to you from your forefathers, but with the precious blood of Christ, a lamb without blemish or defect. He was chosen before the creation of the world, but was revealed in these last times for your sake. Through Him you believe in God, who raised Him from the dead and glorified Him, and so your faith and hope are in God."

1 Peter 1:18–23

Billy Graham tells of a time early in his ministry when he arrived at a small town to preach. He had written a letter back home and wanted to mail it right away. Walking outside, he spotted a small boy standing on the sidewalk and asked him where the post office was. After the boy had given him directions, Mr. Graham thanked him and said, "If you come to my meeting tonight you can hear me tell everyone how to get to heaven!"

"I don't think so," said the boy. "You don't even know how to get to the post office!"

The Bible tells us that Nicodemus was no ordinary citizen. He was a religious Pharisee, a leader of the Jews, a very prominent member of the Sanhedrin. He was a man who committed his life to the study and obedience of the Law. But somehow in all of his teachings and religion, he had missed the message.

In some ways, I can relate to Nicodemus. I wasn't exactly a student of religion, but I did go through confirmation, and I sat in church Sunday after Sunday. I attended Sunday school. In fact, shortly after I was married, I even taught Sunday school. Yet somehow, through all of that, I still missed the message. It wasn't until I was thirty-five years old that God got a hold of my heart, and the message of John 3:16 brought salvation.

Over the centuries, I think there are many people who find themselves in the same position as Nicodemus and me. They get involved in a church but not with Christ. Religion cleans them up and makes them look good, but they have never had a close encounter of the divine kind!

Here we have the biblical *Nick at Night* story. Imagine if you will, Nick as he was walking down the street, having a conversation with himself.

> "I don't get it! We sent some of our people to talk to this John the Baptist, and he just keeps on baptizing people. Doesn't he know that it's not right? The only person that needs to be baptized is a heathen who converts to Judaism. And, they are trying to say that this is some kind of new religion? Impossible! The Law is all that anyone needs. These great principles given to us by God have been defined down to strict laws and rules, which anyone can understand and obey. Why, we can't allow them to just interpret these principles in their own way and change our laws, it's just not right! No, no, no! The Law, as it is defined by the Sanhedrin, is the only way to know God! I certainly don't understand this man called Jesus either! I think he must be a prophet of God to teach with such authority and conviction. He has done so many wonderful miracles, yet, so much of what he does goes against our rules and traditions. I certainly don't understand why he got so angry the other day at the Temple. The merchants were just doing their job after all. The people need sacrifices, and the temple needs the money to operate! It's not like we were playing bingo or anything! Maybe I just need to talk to Jesus myself. Maybe I need to understand where he's coming from. Maybe he really is sent from God. Maybe, just maybe, he really does have the answer to the eternal life question."

Like many other people, Nick's life has been turned upside down. And perhaps for the first time in a long time he has more questions than answers. Today we would call him a "seeker." In the conversation Nick has with Jesus, we can perhaps see a bit of ourselves. We know there is a lack of understanding, because Nicodemus insists on making logical sense to what Jesus says. "How can a man be born when he is old?" Of course, Jesus is speaking on a spiritual level, while Nick is still in the physical realm of things.

Sometimes we try to reason and make sense of God logically; we try to figure out this whole Christianity thing, as if it is lived according to a set of rules and regulations and traditions. We try to fashion Christians into a mold that we have created, and when we do that we not only limit our faith, we limit God.

Nicodemus says, "We know you must be from God, because no one could perform these miraculous signs you are doing unless God were with him." Listen, if we need signs, miracles, and wonders as proof that God exists then we are missing all that God is! Oh, and by the way, just as a side note, remember that Satan is capable of counterfeit miracles too; So be alert!

Instead of getting into a theological debate with Nick over who he is, Jesus, who knows every man's heart, goes right to the heart of the matter: "I tell you the truth; unless a man is born again he cannot see the kingdom of heaven."

Now I want you to see this from two perspectives; one is the perspective of truth. We cannot get into heaven unless we are born again, which has everything to do with our salvation and eternal life and was the real point. The second is the perspective of putting the emphasis on the word *see.* "Unless a man is born again he cannot *see* the kingdom of heaven." He cannot see it. He cannot comprehend it, understand it, or even logically and reasonably talk about it! The Bible says, "The things of the Spirit are foolishness to those who are without the Spirit." In other words, unless a person has heard God's Word, read God's Word, has been convicted and given understanding from God's Holy Spirit, and is born again, he does not have the proper perspective on spiritual things. That's why this was so confusing to Nicodemus, and why it is still confusing to those who are not yet "born again." They have a wrong perspective.

Jesus further explains that "unless a man is born of water" (physical birth) and "born of the Spirit" (spiritual birth: "born again"), "he cannot enter the kingdom of God." Notice the first time he said "cannot see the kingdom," now he says "cannot enter the kingdom."

Nick was perhaps a very moral character; but morality won't do it. He held a very prestigious and distinguished position. But I want you to know that even being a pastor in a church doesn't mean you are saved any more than being in a garage makes you a car! Social position or church position won't get you in. Popularity won't do it. Being rich and famous won't cut it! Your heritage and upbringing? Nope. This "new birth" is not about anything we have, we are, or we do; it is something God does! We need only accept it by faith. In this chapter, we are going to find out what it means to be a *whosoever,* which is very important; because to have eternal life, which was really the question on Nick's mind and heart, is to become a "whosoever!"

Finally, rather than confuse the issue any further, Jesus puts it plain and simple with something Nicodemus would surely understand. Nicodemus, who knew and taught from the Pentateuch, which are the first five books written by Moses, would surely understand this. "Look Nick," says Jesus, "Just as Moses lifted up the snake in the desert, so the Son of Man must be lifted up, that everyone who believes in Him may have eternal life" (John 3:14). "For God did not send his Son into the world to condemn the world, but to save the world through Him" (John 3:17).

Do you think old Nicodemus ever got it? Ultimately, to be born again is not something to be examined or explained, it is something to be experienced! Nicodemus was a member of the Sanhedrin, a Pharisee, who had a close encounter with Jesus. Was his life transformed? Well, in John 19:38, following the crucifixion, it says this: "Later, Joseph of Arimathea asked Pilate for the body of Jesus. Now Joseph was a disciple of Jesus, but secretly because he feared the Jews. With Pilate's permission, he came and took the body away." Then comes verse thirty-nine: "he was accompanied by Nicodemus, the man who had earlier visited Jesus at night." That tells me that the message Jesus proclaimed to Nick that night got through! I think that Nick became a "whosoever" that very night that he came to Jesus.

As we continue, I will be taking a very close, almost word by word, look at John 3:16 and, before we are done, I pray that you will know that you have eternal life. "But these things are written that you may believe that Jesus is the Christ, the Son of God, and that by believing you may have life in His name!" (John 20:31).

But, as you will see, this is only the beginning of the wonderful journey to which God has called you. There is so much more to learn and understand that it takes a lifetime!

Part 1:

FOR GOD—AND ONLY GOD!

I believe this to be the greatest verse in the entire Bible. It is the best-loved and best-known verse by Christians and non-Christians alike. There are only twenty-five words in this verse, yet no other single verse in all the Scriptures has been as blessed in the salvation of so many souls. Martin Luther called John 3:16 the "miniature gospel." It has been called the gospel in a nutshell. It has been called a love letter from God, written in blood, and addressed to all. If ever there was a verse that Satan would love to blot out of the Bible, it would be John 3:16. If ever there was a verse that makes hell tremble, it is John 3:16. If ever there was a verse that has enlightened the path to heaven for multitudes of people, it is John 3:16.

Some have divided the verse into parts like: God's Grace: "For God so loved the world;" God's Gift: "That he gave his only begotten Son;" God's Gospel: "That whosoever believes in Him;" and God's Glory: "shall have everlasting life." There are many ways to look at this verse, but for the sake of this teaching, I simply want to look at the words, beginning with "For God."

Charles Simeon was a British pastor, who every Friday afternoon would entertain the upper classmen of Cambridge who were contemplating the ministry. It was a time when he would share his thoughts and give instruction and advice to the students. At one of these meetings, Simeon told the group of the difference between human writings and God's Word:

> It's hard to hesitate or weep upon paper. It is hard to give the tone of love or kindness on paper. But when it comes to divine writing, God gets a hold of our heart, soul, mind, and spirit in a way that we can "feel" his heart. There is no better verse where this is true than John 3:16. If this were the only verse we had, it would be enough.

The atheist says, "There is no God," and denies the existence of God, but John 3:16 simply proclaims his existence, "For God." It is much the same as Genesis 1:1: "In the beginning, God," and that's all that is needed. If we don't believe those simple words of explanation, then there is no sense reading the rest of Scripture.

An atheist was talking to a Christian and was pointing out all the holidays that we celebrate: Easter, Thanksgiving, Christmas, and the National Day of Prayer.

"We atheists don't have any holidays," he said.

The Christian replied, "Why sure you do, it's April Fool's Day!"

Psalm 14:1 says, "A fool says in his heart there is no God."

A Russian astronaut said, after his return from space, "Some people say there is a God out there, but I did not see him. My mind refuses to believe that which no one has ever seen."

To this a pastor replied, "Have you ever seen the Eiffel Tower"?

The astronaut replied, "No, but because I know of others who have seen it, I can believe it exists."

"Oh," said the pastor, "I am beginning to understand your reasoning. Have you ever seen your brain?"

"No," said the astronaut.

"Has anyone else ever seen your brain?" the pastor asked.

"No," replied the astronaut.

To which, the pastor declared, "Then I reckon you have no brain."

The words *For God* simply declare that he is! That is where it must start. "Those who would come to God must first believe that he exists" (Hebrews 11:6). Once again, if we don't believe the first two words, then the rest of John 3:16 is useless.

I looked up the words *God is,* and I found several verses that tell us who and what God is. Not only does the Bible say that "God is" or that he exists, but it also tells us that God is the Alpha and the Omega, the beginning and the end; God is holy; God is merciful; God is our salvation; God is true and faithful; God is spirit; God is our portion (or supplier); God is light; God is life; and God is love! All of these declare that "he is!"

I have heard that there are some people who

believe God exists, but see him as disinterested or disassociated from all that is happening. As if God created and then left us to fend for ourselves, they see him as a God who is out there, somewhere, and who knows if he will ever come back? These may be the same kind of people who say they believe God exists but refuse to believe or obey his Word. Some may have even experienced God in their lives in some way and yet refuse to be transformed or changed in any way by their experience. So in the end, their lives fail to manifest their belief.

In the early days of Ohio, while it was still wild and untamed, a story is told of a young husband and wife who built a little home in the wilderness. They had a little girl, and one day, when she was just passed two years old, she wandered into the woods. Some Indians found her and took her with them. The mother and father hunted for days but to no avail. They tried to live in that little cabin, but they couldn't stand it. There were just too many things to remind them of their little girl. They packed up their things and moved. For fourteen years, they lived with heavy hearts. Then one day, they were at a trading post, when some Indians came with a white girl who had a birthmark on her right shoulder, which identified her as the lost child. The father ran like a madman to see his daughter and tell her that he was indeed her father. She laughed at him. The mother threw her arms around her, but the girl pushed her away. The mother was devastated. Then she remembered something, and she began to sing the lullaby she sang to her daughter in the cradle. The girl raised her eyes, as if in a dream; as she heard a voice from long ago she realized the truth and ran into her mother's arms.[1]

In the beginning of time, God created mankind. But man was carried away, captive by Satan. Nevertheless, God, in his love, has sought after his children with a passion in his heart to deliver them from their captor. He reaches out to us and says, "I am your Father. I created you, and I love you!" But, many in our world react like the little girl. They laugh, they ridicule, and they push him away. They have been in captivity so long; they won't or can't believe it to be true. It is God's desire to save us from our captor and restore the relationship that has long been broken.

He that comes to God must first believe that he exists. Some might say that this is the hardest part. This is the area that we all struggle with. This is the thing that we all doubt at some time. But the fact is that it is easier to believe God exists than to disbelieve it. The light, truth, and knowledge from God, and of God, are streaming all around us. The Bible says that all we need to do is open our eyes. In fact, in Romans 1, it says that we are "without excuse" for God's "invisible qualities, his eternal power, and divine nature have been clearly seen, being understood from what has been made."

It is amazing to me that children have no problem believing God exists. They have a simple faith, which has not yet learned to reason or doubt. Do you know that it requires long and great effort to train the mind to reject the evidence for the existence of God? But faith is easy. Faith is the combination of the physical senses—the heart, soul, and spirit—convincing the mind of truth. This is why the Bible says that "Without faith, it is impossible to please God." (Hebrews 11:6) It starts with a simple faith, the faith of a mustard seed, and faith in two words, "For God."

Part 2:

SO LOVED

"For this reason I kneel before the Father, from whom his whole family in heaven and on earth derives its name. I pray that out of his glorious riches He may strengthen you with power through His Spirit in your inner being, so that Christ may dwell in your hearts through faith. And I pray that you, being rooted and established in love, may have power, together with all the saints, to grasp how wide and long and high and deep is the love of Christ, and to know this love that surpasses knowledge—that you may be filled to the measure of all the fullness of God."

Ephesians 3:14–19

John 3:16 is the message of God's love, which was shown through his Son, Jesus, who left his glory for the cross of Calvary that "whosoever believes in him shall not perish but have ever-lasting life." This best known verse has been called "an ocean of thought in a drop of language."

We have looked at the first two words, *For God.* "Anyone who comes to Him must first believe that He exists." That's what we call *faith.* Although we have not seen God, we have felt and experienced his presence in our lives and in nature itself, and that's enough for us to believe!

Now, we will look at the next two words, *so loved.* There is an old Hymn by F.M. Lehman in which the last stanza goes like this: Could we with ink the ocean fill; and the skies - of parchment made;/Were every stalk on earth a quill; and every man a scribe by trade;/ to write the love ... of God above ... would drain the ocean dry."[2] In Ephesians 3, we read the prayer of Paul that the saints at Ephesus will have the "power, together with all the saints, to grasp how wide, and long, and high, and deep is the love of Christ, and to know this love that surpasses (is greater than and of greater value than) knowledge; that you may be filled to the measure of all the fullness of God" (18–19). So as we think of these two words *so loved,* let's consider these four things: the width, the length, the height, and the depth of God's love.

First of all, the width of God's love has no confinements. The love of God is without boundaries. It is not limited in any way. In fact, John 3:16 tells us that his love is a *whosoever* love. It is not limited racially, nationally, politically, socially, or personally. It says that "God so loved the *world*"—that's everyone! Everyone who has ever lived, is living, and ever will live. The width of God's love has no confinements. Unlike God, it has been said that people have enough religion to cause them to hate sin but not enough to love one another! A *whosoever* love has no confinements.

Second, the length of God's love has no conclusion. God said in Jeremiah 31:3, "Yea I have loved Thee with an everlasting love." You can go as far as you wish into the past to a time before a star ever shone in the sky, a leaf ever fluttered in the breeze, or the first wave ever washed upon the beach, and you will be no nearer the beginning of God's love than you are right now! And if you project your mind as far as you possibly could into eternity future to a time when mountains are turned to dust, or the sun has grown cold, and the pages of his judgment book begin to unfold, you will be no nearer the end of God's love than you are right now. The point is that there is never a time when God does not love us. The length of *whosoever* love has no conclusion.

Third, the height of God's love has no comparison. In Webster's dictionary, *love* is described as "a tender passionate affection; a feeling of warm personal attachment; a strong liking for something." These all seem to describe some kind of feeling, but the truth is that these feelings are the *effects* or the *fruit* of love. You can no more define the essence of love than you can define the essence of God. However, while love may be difficult to describe, it is easy to demonstrate. It is probably true that there is no greater demonstration of love, in this world at least, than a mother's love. A mother's love is even greater than a father's, because of the very fact that a child is literally part of the woman's body as it grows until birth. A mother loves unconditionally and unceasingly.

There is also a love between a man and a woman that brings out and even intensifies all the things described by Webster. But, as deep as these loves are, they cannot be a measuring stick for God's love, because God's love transcends and surpasses all human love. Try as we may, we can find no real comparison for the love of God toward his creation. A *whosoever* love has no comparison.

And finally, the depth of God's love has no conditions. You see, so often our love is inspired and motivated by love we receive. It is a matter of *reciprocation.* In fact, our love for Christ is motivated by the fact that he first loved us and gave himself for us. Furthermore, we love those who, in our mind's eye, are desirable and deserving. There are certain features, certain qualities, and certain virtues that spark our love. At the same time, the absence of these virtues keeps us from loving.

When we think of God's love, we are to be mindful that there is nothing in us or about us to attract his love. In fact, we are depraved and disgraceful sinners! Every one of us! "For all have sinned and come short of the glory of God" (Romans 3:23). If anything, you might think there is more about sinful man that would attract the wrath of God. But, in spite of who we are and what we are, God still loves us without conditions.

God does not demand that we be certain kind of persons, that we look a certain way, or that we posses certain qualities. We may demand these things, but we don't have to be lovable to be loved by God! He just loves us! And the great thing is that when we love him back, he helps us to become lovable to those around us! A *whosoever* love has no conditions.

There was a man named Nanson who was looking for the North Pole. Each day while in his ship, he gathered up rope and let down a weight to measure the depth of the ocean. One day he came to a place where the water was exceptionally deep, and he could not sound the bottom. In his ledger he wrote down the length of his rope and then wrote "deeper than that!"[3] Whatever I have said in this chapter about God's love, know this—it's deeper than that!

"For God so loved the world that He gave his only begotten Son, that whosoever believes in Him shall not perish but have everlasting life." It is a love that is so wide, it has no confinements, its length has no conclusion, and its height has no comparison and is so deep that it has—no . . . oh, wait a minute. I'm sorry, according to this verse, there is one condition: You must be a *whosoever!* You see, it says, "whosoever believes." You must be a believer! God's acceptance of us depends on our acceptance of him.

If you don't know or have not felt or experienced God's love in your life, I invite you to become a *whosoever* today!

Part 3:

WHAT IN THE WORLD IS THE WORLD?

In this scripture, *world* is mentioned some sixteen times.

> "After Jesus said this, He looked toward heaven and prayed: "Father, the time has come. Glorify your Son, that your Son may glorify you. For you granted Him authority over all people that He might give eternal life to all those you have given Him. Now this is eternal life: that they may know you, the only true God, and Jesus Christ, whom you have sent. I have brought you glory on earth by completing the work you gave me to do. And now, Father, glorify me in your presence with the glory I had with you before the *world* began. I have revealed you to those whom you gave me out of the *world.* They were yours; you gave them to me and they have obeyed your word. Now they know that everything you have given me comes from you. For I gave them the words

you gave me and they accepted them. They knew with certainty that I came from you, and they believed that you sent me. I pray for them. I am not praying for the *world*, but for those you have given me, for they are yours. All I have is yours, and all you have is mine. And glory has come to me through them. I will remain in the *world* no longer, but they are still in the *world*, and I am coming to you. Holy Father, protect them by the power of your name—the name you gave me—so that they may be one as we are one. While I was with them, I protected them and kept them safe by that name you gave me. None has been lost except the one doomed to destruction so that Scripture would be fulfilled. I am coming to you now, but I say these things while I am still in the *world*, so that they may have the full measure of my joy within them. I have given them your word and the *world* has hated them, for they are not of the *world* any more than I am of the *world*. My prayer is not that you take them out of the *world* but that you protect them from the evil one. They are not of the *world*, even as I am not of it. Sanctify them by the truth; your word is truth. As you sent me into the *world*, I have sent them into the *world*. For them I sanctify myself, that they too may be truly sanctified. My prayer is not for them alone. I pray also for those who will believe in me through their message, that all of them may be one, Father, just as you are in me and I am in you. May they also be in us so that the *world* may believe that you have sent me. I have given them the glory that you gave me, that they may be one as we are one: I in them and you in me. May they be brought to complete unity

> to let the *world* know that you sent me and have loved them even as you have loved me.
>
> Father, I want those you have given me to be with me where I am, and to see my glory, the glory you have given me because you loved me before the creation of the *world.* Righteous Father, though the *world* does not know you, I know you, and they know that you have sent me. I have made you known to them, and will continue to make you known in order that the love you have for me may be in them and that I myself may be in them."
>
> John 17:1–26

So far in this chapter, we have considered the first four words of John 3:16. *For God:* Those that come to him must first believe that he exists. *So Loved:* We try to grasp how wide, how high, how long, and how deep is the love of God. Now, we are going to look at the next two words—*the world*—and try to discover what in the world is the world?

In the Bible we read, God is the Creator, the sustainer, and the judge of the world; Christ is the Savior of the world, the light of the world, and the reconciler of the world. It says that we Christians were chosen out of the world; we are sent into the world, are not to be conformed to the world, nor corrupted by the world; we are to be separate from the world, yet we are to be the salt and light of the world; and as if that isn't confusing enough, it also says that we were once of the world, but now we are not of the world! So, what in the world is the world?

Well, in the Bible, there are three different and separate meanings for the *world.* Unless we know the difference, it's easy to get confused as to what Scripture is saying.

First of all, the world is a *place.* It's a place we call Earth, third rock from the sun. "Go Ye into all the *world,* and preach the Gospel" (Mark 16:15). "For all these things do the nations of the *world* seek after" (Luke 12:30). "He was in the *world* and the *world* was made by Him." (John 1:9). All of these, of course, speak of this planet on which we live.

It was (a) *created by God.* God is the designer and the architect of this world and the universe in which it spins. In John 1:3 it says, "All things were made by him and without him was not anything made." It is (b) *controlled by God.* We read in Colossians 1:16, "For by him were all things created, that are in heaven and that are on the earth, visible and invisible whether they be thrones or dominions, or principalities, or powers; all things were created by him and for him; and he is before all things, and by him all things consist." The word *consist* literally means "to hold together." He is the one who holds it all together! God is the glue of the galaxies! We look at our great planet and realize that it revolves on its axis, travels around the sun, and is circled by the moon and all the other planets in their orbits with their own moons, and it does not lose more than a second of time every one hundred years. How can that be? How can it be so accurate? Easy, God is in control!

Second, the world is a *program.* It is a system of things that exists. For instance, we talk about the "wide world of sports" or the "world of politics." We are not talking about a planet of sports or a planet of politics (although some politicians seem to be from another planet!), but we are talking about a program, a system. So when we read about the "prince of this world," the "cares of this world," or the "wisdom of this world" or, as in our Scripture, the fact that we are not "part of this world" does not mean that we are some kind of aliens from another planet but that we are not a part of the world's program or system. This means we are no longer part of the world's way of thinking and doing things. But rather we are part of God's program, God's system, and God's way of thinking and doing things!

This world's system or program is going in a direction opposite of God. It is a deliberate program on a deliberate course, and it has a deliberate leader! His name is Satan. This is why we read things like, "For our struggle is not with flesh and blood, but against the rulers and authorities and powers of this dark world" (Ephesians 6:12). The *world* in this sense is a program to keep men, women, and children away from God.

Third, the world is a *people.* It is a group of people who are lost without God. The Bible classifies people into two categories: lost and saved. Those who are lost, the Bible tells us are also condemned and "dead" in trespasses and sin. The lost of this *world*—whether planet or system or people—need to be saved! And so, there is good news; "For God so loved the world."

People may be caught up in the world's system, they may be lost, but they don't have to stay that way.

Let's look at 2 Corinthians 5:14–6:1:

> "For Christ's love compels us, because we are convinced that one died for all, and therefore all died. And He died for all, that those who live should no longer live for themselves but for Him who died for them and was raised again. So from now on we regard no one from a worldly point of view. Though we once regarded Christ in this way, we do so no longer. Therefore, if anyone is in Christ, He is a new creation; the old has gone, the new has come! All this is from God, who reconciled us to Himself through Christ and gave us the ministry of reconciliation that God was reconciling the world to Himself in Christ, not counting men's sins against them. And He has committed to us the message of reconciliation. We are therefore Christ's ambassadors, as though God were making his appeal through us. We implore you on Christ's behalf: Be reconciled to God. God made Him who had no sin to be sin for us, so that in Him we might become the righteousness of God."

God loves his creation—all the planets of the universe and everything in the universe. And he especially loves his people. That's true. However, God hates the world's system and programs, which draw his creation away from him. But we must know that he will never draw away from his Creation. He loves us so much that he gave his only Son. He offered up his only Son, "That whosoever believes in him shall not perish but have everlasting life." We have a lot more to look at in this wonderful verse of scripture. It's not enough just to believe in God. It's not even enough to believe in God and know that he loves us. We need to know that there is even more.

Part 4:

GOD'S GREATEST GIFT

We have looked at the words *For God* in part one, *So Loved* in part two, and *The World* in part three, and now we are going to focus in on the words *he gave his only Son.* In his Word, we can find that God has given us many things, but his greatest gift of all was his Son.

When it comes to giving, there are thousands of stories that could be told and thousands more that could be preached, but there is only one story of giving that has eternal value: "he gave his only Son."

A little girl was given two dollars by her father. He told her that she could do anything she wanted with one, but the other was to be given to God in church on Sunday. The girl nodded in agreement and asked if she could go to the candy store. With visions of all that she could buy with her dollar, she skipped happily down the street. Just then, she tripped and fell down; the wind blew one of her dollars into a storm drain. Picking herself up and dusting herself off, she looked at the dollar still in her hand, then looked at the drain, and said, "Well, Lord, there goes your dollar!"[4]

When it comes to giving, the story is told of the wealthy Texan who was in the habit of giving his dad some pretty expensive and rather unique gifts for Father's Day. One year it was lessons in hang gliding; another year it was a deep sea fishing trip. But this particular year he had purchased a very rare, talking bird that could speak five languages and sing the *Yellow Rose of Texas!* The bird cost a thousand dollars, but his father was worth every cent. About a week after Father's Day, he called his dad to see how he liked the bird. "It was delicious!" said his father.[5]

Well, we have all heard of stories of philanthropists who have given money for many worthy causes. Does anyone remember the newspaper column by Percy Ross, where people would actually write in and ask for money for some reason? Sometimes these stories impress or inspire us, but there is no greater story of giving than John 3:16.

I want to look at God's gift to us from three perspectives. The first is that God's gift of his Son was *expressive.* Whenever we give gifts to anyone, that gift is always expressive of certain feelings. For example, we may give to express appreciation. We may give to express our consideration, such as a thinking-of-you type card. Many times we give to express our sympathy for someone's loss. At other times, we give to express our love, like Valentine's Day. Gifts are *expressive.* God's gift was expressive and motivated by his love. He was sending a message to the whole world. A message that said, "I love you! I love you enough to do that, which you cannot do on your own! I love you enough to send the very best!"

Ephesians 2:8 says, "For it is by grace you have

been saved, through faith and not of yourselves, it is the *gift* of God—Not by works, so that no one can boast." God freely gave an expressive gift of his love and provided the only way of salvation.

Second, God's gift of his Son was *expensive.* God freely gave, and we can freely receive. However, it should never be misunderstood that this gift was without cost. For some people, the expense of the gift is equated with the measure of the love. Humanly, this is not always true. But if that were the case, then God's love is the greatest you will ever know! It cost Jesus his life. He said, in John 15:13, "No greater love hath man than he lay down his life for his friends."

Crucifixion was the worst possible way to die, yet he was willing to give his life for ours. He came from the adoration of heaven to the abominations of the earth, from the coronations of heaven to the condemnations of the earth; he came from the majesty of heaven to the misery of the earth; he came from praise to persecution. "No greater love hath a man for his friends"; it was an *expensive* gift.

Thirdly, God's gift of his Son was an *essential* gift. Why was it essential? Because God's pronouncement on the human race was Romans 3:10: "There is none righteous, not even one," and in 3:23, "All have sinned and come short of the glory of God." The condition of sin and sinfulness in man brought condemnation. Man violated the law of God, and the price was not only physical death but eternal death. Because man is a sinner by birth, a sinner by nature, and a sinner by choice, the gift of God through Jesus his Son was an *essential* gift. Romans 8:32 says that God "spared not his own Son" that we might live! He is the only way to the Father.

The story is told of a keeper of a drawbridge over a great river. He suddenly heard the thunder of an approaching train and noticed that the drawbridge was open. At the same time, his child who was playing nearby rolled down a sharp embankment into the wild water of the river. The man knew, that if he plunged into the water to save his child, the drawbridge would not be closed, and a trainload of passengers would plunge to their deaths. If he stayed and closed the drawbridge, his child would drown. He hesitated for a moment and then swung the drawbridge into place. Then he jumped into the river and pulled out his dead son.[6]

The Apostle Paul said in 2 Corinthians 5:21, "For he hath made him to be sin for us, who knew no sin; that we might be made the righteousness of God in him."

For God so loved the world, that He gave his only Son.

A certain medieval monk announced he would be preaching next Sunday evening on "The Love of God." As the shadows fell and the light ceased to come in through the cathedral windows, the congregation gathered. In the darkness of the altar, the monk lit a candle and carried it to the crucifix. First of all, he illumined the crown of thorns; next, the two wounded hands; and then the marks of the spear wound. In the hush that fell, he blew out the candle and left the chancel. There was nothing else to say.[7]

In Chicago, during the Great Depression, there was a little boy who sold newspapers on the street corner to help provide for his family. His tattered jacket, which was about three sizes too small, provided little relief from the bitter-winter, Chicago wind.

On one particularly cold day, the young man was nearly frostbitten when a policeman approached him. "Son, do you know that big, white house on the corner a couple of blocks up?"

"Yes, sir, I pass it every day on my way to this corner," said the lad.

"Well, I want you to walk over there, step up onto the porch, and knock on the door. When the lady that lives there answers the door, just say, John 3:16."

The young man did as he was told. He walked up to the door and knocked. A kind face appeared at the door, and the boy looked up and said, "John 3:16." The gentle lady opened the door wide and invited the cold, shivering, dirty little boy to come into the living room where there was a roaring fire blazing in the fireplace. As he sat there, getting warm and cozy, he said to himself, "John 3:16; I don't understand it, but it sure does make a cold little boy warm!"

Soon that lady came out and led the boy into the dining room where there was a feast of all the foods that he loved. She sat him down and he began to eat. He ate until he couldn't stuff another bite in his mouth, and then he said to himself, "John 3:16; I don't understand it, but it sure does make a hungry little boy full!"

After he had eaten, the kind woman took him up to a huge bathroom with a large bathtub filled with water and bubbles. "You take a nice bath and then put on these pajamas," she told him. As the young man sat in the first bath he had in quite a long time and scrubbed through the layers of dirt, he said to himself, "John 3:16; I don't understand it, but it sure does make a dirty little boy clean!"

After his bath the lady brought him to a bedroom, which had the biggest bed he had ever seen. He laid down and immediately fell fast asleep. In the morning, he awoke to the smells of his favorite breakfast. As he was getting dressed in the clothes the woman had laid out for him, the boy said to himself, "John 3:16; I don't understand it, but it sure does give a tired little boy rest!"

He went downstairs, and the table was once again filled with food that he loved. After breakfast, the kind, gentle lady led the boy back into the living room and in front of the fire. She took her Bible and began to explain to him about the love of God and Jesus' dying on the cross. The little boy accepted God's gift of everlasting life that day. Then he said to himself, "John 3:16: Now I understand it. It makes a lost little boy saved!"[8]

Part 5:

WHOSOEVER BELIEVES

"When Jesus came to the region of Caesarea Philippi, He asked his disciples, "Who do people say the Son of Man is?" They replied, "Some say John the Baptist; others say Elijah; and still others, Jeremiah or one of the prophets." "But what about you?" He asked. "Who do you say I am?" Simon Peter answered, "You are the Christ, the Son of the living God."

Matthew 16:13–16

We have been breaking down this verse into specific parts in order to gain more insight into the simplicity as well as the depth of this one verse. It is the entire Gospel condensed into one verse, and in this verse, we have looked at the words *For God* and only God, none other than God, and the God in whom we must believe exists before anything else is true; *so loved,* a love that is so wide, so high, so deep that we can hardly fathom it; *the world,* that which is a place, a system, and a people; *that He gave his only son,* God's greatest gift, a free gift, an expressive gift, an expensive gift, and an essential gift; and now, *whosoever believes in Him.*

I want to go back and bring out a couple of things I didn't mention previously in this verse. I have always thought that of all our earthly hymns, which might be sung in heaven, "Holy, Holy, Holy" would top the list:

> Holy, holy, holy! Lord God Almighty!
>
> Early in the morning our song shall rise to thee.
>
> Holy, holy, holy! Merciful and mighty,
>
> God in three persons, blessed Trinity!

We need to know that the Trinity—God the Father, Jesus the Son, and the Holy Spirit—all are involved in our salvation. God the Father "gave" his only Son. It was, as we are told in this great verse, because of his great love for his creation that he was willing to do for us that which we could not do ourselves. Jesus, God's only Son, was willing to be given! He endured the cross; he took upon himself the sins of the world that we might be reconciled, saved, and born-again through his sacrifice. The Holy Spirit was involved from the beginning when the angel came to Mary and told her she would bear a child. She was told that the Holy Spirit would come upon her and the one born to her would be the Son of God. The Holy Spirit is involved in our salvation by divine inspiration, by revelation, and by the work of conviction. The Bible is very clear about these three things: (1) God is willing to save us, (2) God wants to save us, and (3) God is waiting to save us.

"It is God's will that not even one should perish, but all would come to repentance." (2nd. Peter 3:9)

However, the Bible is also clear that the choice is up to you and me. God is willing to save, wanting to save, and waiting to save "whosoever believes!" Do you know that the most wonderful word in the Bible is *whosoever?* You see, God is not just the God of the Jews; he's the God of "whosoever believes." Jesus is not the Savior of a select few or chosen few, he is the Savior of "whosoever believes." The Holy Spirit is not the power behind just preachers, evangelists, and a few selected and called people; the Holy Spirit is the power behind *whosoever believes.*

In John 4:13 (KJV), Jesus told the woman at the well, "*Whosoever* drinketh of this water shall thirst again: But *whosoever* drinketh of the water that I shall give him shall never thirst, but the water that I shall give him shall be in him a well of water springing up into everlasting life."

In John 12:46 (KJV) he says, "I am come a light into the world, that *whosoever* believeth on me should not abide in darkness." In Acts 2:21 (KJV), "And it shall come to pass, that *whosoever* shall call upon the name of the Lord shall be saved" "Whosoever will," "Whosoever believes," and "Whosoever comes"—that is anyone who *chooses* to come! Understand this: God cannot and will not do anything in your life, until you choose to become a *whosoever!* Oh, he will do a lot of things to guide and change your circumstances and so on and continuously try to bring you to a point of decision, but it is you who must decide!

Understand also, even though God's offer is for whosoever, there is one condition. Anyone can come, but they must come on God's terms and not their own. Let me explain what I mean by that. Anyone can be saved, but it is important to remember that there is only one way to be saved. Whosoever believes *in him.* It does not say whosoever lives a good life, whosoever keeps the Ten Commandments or whosoever goes to church and is baptized. It says, "Whosoever believes in him!" There are not several ways to get to heaven; there is only one: Jesus Christ, the way, the truth, and the life. No one comes to the Father except by him. "There is no other name under heaven by which we must be saved" (Acts 4:12).

Listen to the words of John again in his first letter:

> "Anyone who believes in the Son of God has this testimony in his heart. Anyone who does not believe, God has made him out to be a liar, because he has not believed the testimony God has given about His Son. And this is the testimony; God has given us eternal life, and this life is in his Son. He who has the Son has life; he who does not have the Son of God does not have life."
>
> 1 John 5:10

In John 20:31, it says, "But these are written, that ye might believe that Jesus is the Christ, the Son of God; and that believing ye might have life through his name." There is only one way to know that you have eternal life; you must be a *whosoever.*

When the Lord Jesus explained the new birth to Nicodemus that night, he referred to the Old Testament story of Moses lifting up the brazen serpent as a cure for poisonous snake bites. There, in Numbers 21:9, we are told, "So Moses made a bronze snake and put it up on a pole. Then when anyone was bitten by a snake and looked at the bronze snake, he lived." Compare this with the new birth passage where twice in two connecting verses (John 3:15 and 16) Jesus told Nicodemus—who was a religious man, a churchgoer, by the way—whosoever believes! Yes, whosoever believes. It is that broad—and that definite—in its offer.

Someone once told of a man who, for whatever reasons, felt Christ would not receive him. He lamented, "I am such a miserable, wicked, helpless sinner; there is no hope for me. I have tried to get saved, praying and resolving, but it is no use."

He was asked, "Do you believe, as the Word of God says, that Christ died for our sins and rose again for our justification?"

"Of course I do," he said.

He was asked, "What would you do if Jesus were here on Earth in the flesh again now?"

The man responded with enthusiasm, "I would go to him at once!"

He was asked, "What would you say?"

"I would tell him that I am a lost sinner, and I would ask him to save me," the man said.

"And how do you think he would respond?"

Instead of replying, the man simply stood silently for several moments. Then, the poor sinner looked up, a smile breaking across his face, and he softly replied,

"He would say, 'I will.' And he went away rejoicing with joy unspeakable and full of glory.[9]

The second verse of the old Hymn "Whosoever Will" reads:

"Whosoever cometh need not delay;

Now the door is open, enter while you may;

For Jesus is the true, and only living way."

"Whosoever will, may come."[10]

You can't become a *whosoever* after you are gone. Once you are dead and gone, you will have made your choice. Why not make that choice today? In my church, I have passed out some colorful buttons that say "I'm a whosoever!" Friends, we need to wear this button with assurance and joy! We know what it means, and we know what to tell those who ask what it means?

Part 6:

SHALL NOT PERISH

Job 14:14 asks the question: "If a man dies, will he live again?"

Okay, let's get to the last part of this teaching. "For God so loved the world that He gave his only Son, that whosoever believes in him shall not perish but have eternal life." Let's look at those words, *shall not perish.*

I looked up the word *perish,* and it was fascinating. The definition of the word *perish* was "to die through violence or privation; to decay." Now, being as educationally limited as I am, I looked up the word *privation.* It means "a lack of the usual comforts and necessities of life." And, of course, *decay* means to decompose or rot! Now if you put these all together, it would look like this: *to perish* means to die, decompose, or rot, for the lack of the usual comforts and necessities of life! Hold that thought.

For our purpose, we also need to look at the word *life,* because the scripture says that we "shall not perish, but have eternal *life.*" So what are the comforts and necessities of life? *Webster's Dictionary* describes *life* as "the animate existence of an individual." Look up the word *animate,* and you find "to give physical nature or spirit to; or to make alive!" Now we are getting somewhere! Are you okay so far?

Knowing all this, let me then paraphrase John 3:16 this way: "For God so loved the world that He gave his only Son, that whosoever believes in him shall not" die, decompose, or rot due to the lack of the necessities of life; but rather have life - an everlasting, animate, physical existence!

Did you know that the Bible has ten times more to say about hell than it does about heaven? Hell, you see, is a place reserved for those who *perish.* However, heaven is for "whosoever believes in him." Death is inevitable. It is certain. The ratio since the beginning of time is one-to-one! "Man is destined to die once, and after that to face judgment" (Hebrews 9:27). Nothing can prevent it; not wisdom, not wealth, not exercise, not even holiness!

We never know when death will come. Our physical existence on this earth is uncertain. We are a biodegradable species! We are in fact "perishable." But, the good news of John 3:16 is that even though we are perishable, we need not perish! The Apostle Paul in 1 Corinthians 15:50 agrees. "I declare unto you, brothers, that flesh and blood cannot inherit the kingdom of God, nor does the perishable inherit the imperishable." So, how does the perishable become imperishable? How does the mortal put on immortality? John 3:16 is very simple, and it is very clear: "whosoever believes in Him shall not perish!"

Did you realize that according to God's Word, in

Revelation 20:6 and 20:14, there is what is called "the second death?" There is our physical death, death to this physical life here on this earth. And there is the second death, which follows the judgment. Beginning at verse twelve, it says, "Then I saw the dead, great and small, standing before the throne, and books were opened." Now, this is not about Christians. This is not about those who have been "born again" or have become *whosoevers*. This follows the rapture of the church and the wedding supper of the Lamb and the judgment of rewards. These are all those who choose to go to the grave not knowing nor choosing Jesus Christ as their Savior!

It goes on to say,

> "Another book was opened, which is the book of life. The dead were judged according to what they had done as recorded in the books. The sea gave up the dead that were in it, and death and Hades gave up the dead that were in them, and each person was judged according to what he had done. Then death and Hades were thrown into the lake of fire. The lake of fire is the *second death*. If anyone's name was not found written in the book of life, he was thrown into the lake of fire."
>
> Revelation 20:12–15

The great tragedy of hell is that not one person had to go there. I have been looking through the rule book; you don't have to go there! Listen, God loved every single person who is in hell. God gave his Son for every person that is in hell. God offered his free gift of salvation to every person in hell! All they had to do was make the choice to become a *whosoever.* Again, Jesus said: "I am the Way, the Truth, and the Life; no one comes to the Father except by me" (John 14:6). Let me say that again in my own way: the truth is that Jesus is the only way to find life—animate, physical, now life—and life eternal, a forever existence with God.

So the truth of God's Word tells us that we can be born once and die twice, or we can be born twice and die once! Unless of course, Jesus comes to rapture his church, in which case "the dead in Christ shall rise first then we who are alive (and have been born again) will be caught up to meet them in the air" (1 Thessalonians 4:16). Halleluiah!

Part 7:

MORE BEYOND

In Valladolid, Spain, where Christopher Columbus died in 1506, there stands a monument commemorating this great discoverer. Perhaps the most interesting feature of the memorial is a statue of a lion at the base of it where the Spanish National Motto is engraved. The lion reaches out with its paw and is destroying one of the Latin words that had been part of Spain's motto for centuries.

Before Columbus made his voyages, the Spaniards thought they had reached the outer limits of Earth. Thus, their motto was "no more beyond." The word being torn away by the lion is the word *no,* changing the motto, and making it read, "More Beyond." Christopher Columbus had proven that there was indeed more beyond, and the same is true for those that have discovered the truth of God's Word, the Bible. There is more beyond!

Everyone who is born into this world will also have to leave it one day, and for most, our deepest instincts and convictions tell us there is something beyond the grave. This can't be all there is.

In the book of Exodus, chapter sixteen, verse six, there are some awesome words that Moses spoke to the Israelites after crossing the Red Sea, words that still speak to us today. It is a simple, yet powerful verse; it says this: "In the evening, you will know that it was the Lord who brought you out of Egypt, and in the morning you will see the glory of God." I would like to take those words and hold them high above the darkness of the grave. In the morning you shall see the glory of the Lord!

Here in this present human life, we are permitted to see a glimpse of the beauty, a glimpse of truth and goodness, we get a peek at the ultimate plan and meaning of the universe. For some, for those of us who dare to venture into God's Word and God's world, we can get just a portion of the majesty and splendor of God. However, it is but a fraction of what is waiting beyond. There is more beyond! "No eye hath seen, no ear has heard, no mind has conceived what God has prepared for those who love Him" (1 Corinthians 2:9).

In the book of Revelation, chapters twenty-one and twenty-two, we receive a glimpse of God's heavenly city. "Its brilliance is like that of a very precious jewel, like jasper, clear as crystal" (Revelation 21:11). There are twelve gates, and "each gate is made of a single pearl" (21:21). The street of the city was of pure gold with the "river of life flowing from the throne of God and of the Lamb down the middle of the great street of the city. On each side of the river stood the tree of life"(22:1–2); "no longer will there be any curse" (22:3); "no more death, or mourning or crying or pain"

(21:4); "They will see his face," (22:4) "and they shall live and reign forever" (22:5).

Science has shown us that there are things like colors we can't see, such as ultraviolet or infrared. I think in heaven there are colors that man has never seen nor imagined! I say to you this day—there is more beyond!

The curse of life is death. The Bible has only three things to say about death. One is found in the book of Genesis where it says "And the Lord God commanded the man, 'You are free to eat from any tree in the garden; but, you must not eat from the tree of the knowledge of good and evil, for when you eat of it you shall surely die" (Genesis 2:6). Man of course, disobeyed God, which was sin, and the result of sin is the curse of death. The Bible says in Romans 6:23, "The wages of sin is death." There was something else that I must point out in this story; it's found in Genesis chapter three, verse twenty-two.

> "And God said: The man has now become like one of us, knowing good and evil. He must not be allowed to reach out his hand and take also from the tree of life, and eat, and live forever. So The Lord God banished him from the garden, and placed cherubim with a flaming sword flashing back and forth *to guard the way to the tree of life."*

This becomes very important in the end.

The second thing the Bible says about death is that "it is the destiny of every man to die once, and after that to face the judgment" (Hebrews 9:27). We covered that in part six.

The third is rather interesting and probably most important. It comes from the book of Revelation, chapter twenty.

> "And I saw the dead, great and small, standing before the throne, and books were opened. Another book was opened, which is the book of life. The dead were judged according to what they had done as recorded in the books. The sea gave up the dead that were in it, and death and Hades gave up the dead that were in them, and each person was judged according to what he had done. Then death and Hades were thrown into the lake of fire. The lake of fire is the second death. *If anyone's name was not found written in the book of life, he was thrown into the lake of fire."*
>
> Revelation 20:12–15

That's basically all the Bible has to say about death. Death is the result of sin. It's man's destiny to die once. And, if one's name is not found in the Book of Life, we face what is called the "second death." Basically, that's it, because that's all we need to know about death!

You see, the truth is that God's Word is concerned from beginning to end about *life,* not just eternal, spiritual things as some would believe, but even more so with this life, right here, right now. 1 Timothy 4:8, for example, says, "Godliness has value for all things, holding promise for both the *present life* as well as the *life to come.*"

Jesus did not come to tell us all about death and dying. He said "I have come that they may have *life* and have it more abundantly!" (John 10:10). "I am the resurrection and the *life*"

(John 11:25). "I am the Truth, the Way, and the *life*" (John 14:6). And again, he said, "I am the Bread of *life*" (John 6:48). The Apostle John wrote, "These things were written that you may believe and that by believing you may have *life*" (John 20:31).

Let me take you again to Revelation 20 and 21. Remember, man was banished from the garden and no longer had access to the tree of life. Revelation 20 speaks of the Lamb's Book of Life and those whose names are not found in the book face the "second death." I would like to offer you a simple statement once again for your consideration: he who is born once dies twice. But, he who is born twice, dies once! God says it is only destined for man to die once. It is when we reject God and his Word and refuse to be "born again" and to have our name written in the Lamb's Book that we are in fact choosing to die twice!

Now, listen to this from the book of Revelation. "Only those whose names are written in the Lamb's Book of Life" may enter the city (Revelation 21:27b). "Then the angel showed me the river of the water of life as clear as crystal flowing from the throne of God and of the Lamb, down the middle of the great street of the city. *On each side of the river stood . . . the Tree of Life*" (Revelation 22:1–2). Halleluiah! "No longer is there any curse" (Revelation 22:3). We will once again have access to the tree of life, and live and reign with him forever and forever!

In the beginning, God speaks our name, and we

awaken into this life. We find ourselves in the loving arms of someone who knows our every need. When we learn to speak, we call her Mom. The days and years go by, and slowly but surely, we learn the lessons of living (good and bad), and we make decisions and choices (good and bad). Then one day, God speaks our name again, we step from this life into the next, and we find ourselves in the loving care of the one who truly knows our every need, because he created us! And his Word says, "He will wipe every tear from our eyes. There will be no more sickness, no more death, nor crying or pain" (Revelation 21:4). My friends, there is more beyond!

In this life, we are like the chick inside the egg that has no idea whatsoever what the world is like outside of the shell. But, when the time comes, it burst forth from that shell into a whole new world of *life*.

A caterpillar lives the first part of its life crawling on the ground and fulfilling its course in life. Then the caterpillar curls up in a cocoon and seemingly dies. If you open up the cocoon, there is nothing there that resembles the caterpillar, only a gooey gel substance. Then, after a period of time, the cocoon springs to life and out comes a beautiful butterfly. No longer forced to crawl on the ground, it spreads its wings and flies. Changed, and given new life!

Moses once spoke to the people and said "See, I have set before you today life and death, blessings and curses, therefore choose life!" (Deuteronomy 30:19). I say again, there is more beyond. Choose life!

Believe:

GETTING THE FIRST BUTTONHOLE RIGHT!

"And without faith it is impossible to please God, because anyone who comes to Him must believe that He exists and that He rewards those who earnestly seek Him."

Hebrews 11:6

Introduction:

GOD IS (ACCORDING TO HIS WORD)

God is: Lord Almighty, omnipotent King, Lion of Judah, Rock of Ages, Prince of Peace, King of kings, Lord of lords, provider, protector, paternal leader, ruling Lord and reigning King of the entire universe. He is Father, helper, guardian, and God. He is the first and last, the beginning and the end. He is the keeper of Creation and the Creator of all he keeps. God is the architect of the universe and the manager of all times.

He always was, is, and will be: unmoved, unchanged, undefeated, and never undone. He was bruised and brought healing. He was pierced and eased pain. He was persecuted and brought freedom. He was dead and brought life. He is raised and brings power. He reigns and brings peace.

The world can't understand him, the armies can't defeat him, the schools can't explain him, and the leaders can't ignore him. Herod couldn't kill him, the Pharisees couldn't confuse him, and the people couldn't hold him! Nero couldn't crush him. Hitler couldn't silence him. And the New Age can't replace him.

He is light, love, longevity, and Lord. He is goodness, kindness, gentleness, and God. He is holy, righteous, mighty, powerful, and pure. His ways are right. His word is eternal. His will is unchanging. And his mind is on me!

He is my redeemer. He is my Savior. He is my guide. He is my peace. He is my Joy. He is my comfort. He is my Lord, and he rules my life. I serve him because his bond is love, his burden is light, and his goal for me is abundant life!

I follow him, because he is the wisdom of the wise, the power of the powerful, the ancient of days, the ruler of rulers, the leader of leaders, and the sovereign Lord of all that was, is, and is to come.

And if that seems impressive to you, try this for size. His goal is a relationship with *me!* He says he will never leave me, forsake me, mislead me, forget me, or overlook me. When I fall, he lifts me up. When I fail, he forgives me. When I am weak, he is strong. When I am lost, he is the way. When I am afraid, he is my courage. When I stumble, he steadies me. When I am hurt, he heals me. When I am broken, he mends me. When I am blind, he leads me. When I am hungry, he feeds me. When I face trials, he is with me. When I face problems, he provides for me. When I face loss, he comforts me. And, when I face death, he will carry me home!

He is everything for everybody, every where, every time, and in every way. He is God, he is faithful, I am his, and he is mine. My Father in heaven can whip the father of this world, and so if you're wondering why I feel so secure, understand this, it's because:

> I believe God is who he says he is!
> I believe God can do what he says he can do!

Part 1:

I BELIEVE WHO GOD IS

> "You are my witnesses, declares the Lord, and my servant whom I have chosen, so that you may know and believe me and understand that I am he. Before me no god was formed nor will there be one after me. I, even I, am the Lord, and apart from me there is no savior. I have revealed and saved and proclaimed—I, and not some foreign god among you. You are my witnesses, declares the Lord, that I am God!"
>
> Isaiah 43:10–12

Let me begin with this statement: The most powerful, driving force of the Christian faith is the certainty that God is who he says he is! This is where it has to begin, but this is only the beginning. *Unless we get the first button in the right buttonhole, nothing else in life will line up.* When it comes to believing God is who he says he is, we can look first to the names of God, which in turn reveal the character of God, as well as some of the things God can do. We will get into that more in another part of this chapter.

Consider for instance, that the first words of the Bible tell us that God is the "Creator of all things." God is *Yaweh,*"I Am." God is *El-Elyon,* "Most High" or "God in the highest," as the angels proclaimed. God is *Jehovah,* which is translated from the Hebrew meaning "The Lord." (When Lord is in small capital letters in your Bible, it is referring to God. When it is in lowercase letters, it is a title, as in Lord Jesus or Lord Fauntleroy.) God is *Jehovah Jireh,* Our "provider." He is *Jehovah Shalom,* our "peace." John tells us that God is love; not that he loves, but that he *is* love! I won't take the time to list all the names listed in his Word as to who God says he is, except that we must know that he is also Judge and Savior, he is perfect, and he is holy!

According to numerous surveys, fifty percent of the 100 million or so of people who attend church on Sunday don't really have absolute assurance of their salvation. Not that they aren't saved. Oh, they have said it! Done it! Claimed it! But, when asked if they died today, would they be in heaven? Their answer is "I hope so" or "I think so." Is that assurance? Look, do you *hope* there is a God? Do you *think* there is a God? Or do you *believe* God?

Even a greater percentage said they were not really that familiar with the person and the ministry of the Holy Spirit in their lives. We're talking about a survey taken of people who attend church! Only two percent said they regularly share their faith in Christ with others. You see, the reality of God seems far removed from our everyday life. In other words, we Christians have become great at "talking the talk," but our everyday walk is sending the world a signal of "unbelief" and even doubt. It's impossible to be salt, it's impossible to be light, it's impossible to be "on fire" for God, if he's not real in your life and in your walk!

I want you to know that I believe God is who he says he is!

If God is not, then we may as well close all the churches. How many would like to live in a community where there were no churches? There are people outside these walls who think the church has nothing to offer. I would suggest they read the book of Revelation to know what the world would be like without the church.

I want to give you three things that I believe need to be a part of the success of the church and the assurance of every Christian.

First, let's talk about the shield of faith. Whenever Satan tries to tempt us or deceive us or cause us to doubt, we need to raise our shield and use one or all of these statements of faith in this chapter against him, the first being "God is who he says he is!"

God's Word has a lot to say about faith, such as, "Without faith it is impossible to please God" (Hebrews 11:6). We are of course, "saved by faith" (Luke 7:50). It is also because of our faith that we can "approach the throne of God with confidence" (Hebrews 4:16). The Word tells us that there is only "one faith" and encourages "unity" in that faith (Ephesians 4:5), "that faith," being faith in God.

Just in the book of Matthew, we find several references to our faith given by Jesus; in chapter nine, verse twenty-two, he says, "Your faith has healed you." In chapter nine, verse twenty-nine, he says, "according to your faith it will be done unto you." In chapter seventeen, twenty-one, he tells the people, "even if they had a little faith, as a mustard seed, they could move mountains." And finally, in chapter thirteen, verse fifty-eight, it says that he "did not do many miracles in Nazareth because of their lack of faith."

Now, I think we can agree that the words *faith* and *belief* are interchangeable in meaning; so let me give you the opposite of what I just quoted above from scripture, which is also true, because the opposite of a truth is also true.

1. God is pleased when we "believe" him.
2. If we don't believe, we are not saved.
3. If we don't believe God, we cannot even approach his throne.
4. It's a lack of believing God that brings "disunity."
5. Our unbelief obstructs healing.
6. Because of unbelief, nothing is done that could be done.
7. Because of unbelief, we can't even move a mustard seed.
8. If we believed God, he would do many miracles in our midst!

In light of all that, do you think it's important that we believe God is who he says he is? We need to raise the level of our faith, so that in times of trial and temptation, we can raise our shield and say to Satan "I believe God is who he says he is!"

The second thing we can do is to seek to raise our level of sanctification. That's a big word, which simply means we need to seek and practice godliness in our lives. We need to remove those things that are ungodly. In other words, we need to walk the walk. The Apostle Paul tells us that we need to "Take off the old self–and put on the new self" (Colossians 3:9–10). In another place, he says we are to "crucify" the old self, the old nature! That's pretty strong language. But it shows how important it is to live what we believe! It is not about making the old self better; it's about *taking off* and *crucifying* the old self!

In the book of Joshua, when the Israelites were getting ready to cross the Jordan, Joshua says to them in chapter three, verse nine, "Consecrate yourselves, for tomorrow the Lord will do amazing things among you!" I would like the Lord to do some amazing things among us, wouldn't you? I looked up the word *amazing,* and it says, "Beyond the bonds of human power, reason, or expectation." How much faith will it take? More than we have now! How much godliness? More than we have now! Chew on that a little bit, and I'll leave you alone.

The third thing we need to do is experience, testify, and journal "God moments." In Hebrew, they are called *kiros* moments. That means when God does something in your life or you experience God in some way, you need to write it down and tell somebody! Testify to what God has done and is doing to the praise of his glory, for the building up, and edification of the church! I have had so many *kiros* moments in my life, I could fill another book!

I want to tell you that, just because we may have taken a stand and made a statement, it means nothing. It's when we begin to flesh it out, that God is going to do something! I don't know what—and you don't know what he will do—but we will recognize it when it happens! We need to share those *kiros*-God moments in order to grow our faith and help others to grow in theirs. Let me give you just one example from God's Word.

When the Israelites were ready, they took a step of faith into the swollen waters of the river Jordan, and they had a *kiros*-God moment. The hand of God stopped the water, and they crossed on dry ground. Listen to what God told Joshua when they reached the other side. "Choose twelve men from among the people, one from each tribe, and tell them to take up twelve stones from the middle of the Jordan" (Joshua 4:2–3a.). And when they camped that night, it says Joshua took the twelve stones and made a memorial, so when they were asked about the stones, they could say they had experienced a God moment! That's it! That's what it's all about! We need to share those *kiros* moments with one another, as well as with the world.

This chapter is going to be a real challenge to our faith; however, faith unchallenged is faith unchanged! And faith unchanged is dead! *I want to tell you again that I believe God is who he says he is!*

When it comes to believing God is who he says he is, we first need to know *who* God says he is. I wrote of the many names for God, which reveal not only who he is, but also a part of what he says he can do. Those things are called *descriptors*–for example, *Jehovah Jireh,* which means "God our provider."

I also wrote about *faith* being the key component as to how much of God we experience in our lives and in the church. And if we can do it on our own, we don't need God. The more we step out in faith for those things we are unable to do except for the hand of God, the more we will experience God at work; the more we experience God, the more we will be willing to step out in faith!

The Bible says that Jesus didn't do any miracles in Nazareth "because of their lack of faith." So believing who God is really is our faith, and our experiences melding together to bring us to the point of *believing* God; not just believing *in* God, but believing God. When our belief wanes, it is either because of a lack of faith or a lack of experience, or possibly both.

The very first truth we learn about God is found in the first four words of the Bible: "In the beginning, God." In these few words, we learn that our God is eternal in nature. Before time and anything else, there was God. This is what is known as a *declarative* statement. It is a statement, which announces something matter-of-factly. The Bible *declares* that "In the beginning God," sets the stage and sets the tone for everything that follows in his Word. "Those who come to God must first believe he exists!" (Hebrews 11:6)

I like how the Psalmist expresses it in Psalm 90:2, in what he calls the "prayer of Moses:" "Before the mountains were born, or You (you) gave birth to the earth and the world, even from everlasting to everlasting, Thou art God."

God has always existed, and he always will exist. In Isaiah 43:10, God says

> Before Me there was no God formed, and there will be none after me. I, even I, am the Lord, and apart from me there is no Savior. I have revealed, and saved and proclaimed - I, and not some foreign god among you. You are my witnesses, declares the Lord, that *I am God*."

And in chapter forty-four, verse six, he says, "I am the first and I am the last, and there is no God besides Me."

It is difficult for our finite minds to comprehend the eternal nature of God. Until we ourselves are ushered into eternity, we must be content in accepting God's explanation of himself as given to Moses in Exodus 3:14, "I am who I am." God is who he says he is!

When it comes to believing God, there is an old saying that the "proof is in the pudding." In other words, the fact that God can do what he says he can do. As I mentioned, a lot of who God is, is revealed in the list of names given to us in his Word. These not only reveal something about his character, but also something God says he can do. *Jehovah Jireh* - "God provides." So, the proof is in the pudding. If God "can do" then he "is." If he "is" then he "can do!" The two go hand-in-hand. One supports the other.

The prophet Jeremiah understood and was awed by God and his power as revealed in his creation of the universe: "But God made the earth by his power; He founded the world by his wisdom and stretched out the heavens by his understanding" (Jeremiah 10:12).

There are many other things in the Bible that, of course, reveal God to us, but I want to bring out just one important fact about God that we often don't think about, and that is his "goodness." I think if we understand that God always has our good in mind, that in all things God is good, right, and just, it will help us to *believe* God in and for all things.

For example, after the creation of the man in Genesis 2:8–9, God placed him in a garden in Eden. The word *Eden* means "delight" and "pleasure," and that is exactly what God intended for mankind. In Eden, God, *Jehovah Jireh,* provided man with everything necessary for his happiness and well-being. He had abundant food and drink. God gave him a companion so as not to be alone. He gave man purpose and responsibility in caring for God's creation. God also surrounded man with the beauty of his creation and called it the state of Virginia. (Just kidding!)

To satisfy the soul, man had the ability and opportunity to walk and talk with his Maker, each day, like good friends. There was relationship, trust, provision, love, peace, joy, and much more in the garden of Eden. In all this, or through his providence, God revealed his great goodness toward man. But there was another way in which God showed his goodness. God provided guidance and instruction to Adam and Eve. He told them to stay away from the tree of the knowledge of good and evil.

A lot of people don't think of God's instructions and guidance as a manifestation of his goodness. They may see God's commandments and instructions as a manifestation of his morality and his perfect righteousness, which they are, but they do not see the connection between God's commandments and God's goodness. After all, God's commandments are restricting! You can't do this, and you can't do that!

Did God tell Adam and Eve not to eat the forbidden fruit simply because he wanted to keep them from something delicious and satisfying? Or did God prohibit their eating the fruit merely to test their loyalty and obedience? The answer to both questions is an emphatic *no!* God forbade Adam and Eve from partaking of the one tree, because he knew the *consequences.* It would destroy their paradise.

Eating of the fruit would destroy their perfect happiness. Instead of increasing their well-being and satisfaction in life, it would bring some very negative consequences: physical death, mental guilt, emotional fear and shame, and spiritually, it would bring separation and the end of intimate fellowship with God.

God does not make rules just for the sake of making rules. He's not a bureaucrat on some power trip, who makes rules and regulations simply because he has the authority to do so. God does not lay down commandments and instructions to keep us from having fun. His guidance is for our good. His instruction is for our good and for the good of others around us. So is some-thing good because God commands it, or does God command it because it is good? The answer to both is yes. God will never go against his character or his Word. God is who he says he is. Fortunately for Adam and Eve and us, their offspring, God is not only a good and just God, but he is also a God of infinite mercy and bountiful grace. God demonstrated these traits, even while punishing the first couple. We see his mercy by making it *impossible* for Adam and Eve to eat again from the Tree of Life. In Genesis chapter three, he banished them from Eden where the Tree of Life grew. Why should this be seen as a display of God's mercy, love, and goodness? Well, by eating the fruit of the Tree of Life, one becomes immortal. Think of living forever with a body that is subject to pain, sickness, and disease. Ponder living forever with guilt, shame, fear, disappointment, sadness, and discouragement. Consider how it would be to live forever in a world of crime, oppression, betrayal, hatred, strife, and war. We all yearn for immortality. We all wish to live and never die; however, *not* under those circumstances.

God, as well, did not want that for Adam and Eve or for us. Thus, in mercy, he made sure that such a tragedy would never take place. However, the good news is that in Revelation 22, we find that in the end, we get it all back! In his letters to the churches, in chapter two of the book of Revelation, Jesus says: "To him who overcomes, I will give the right to eat from the Tree of Life, which is in the paradise of God" (Revelation 2:7). "Without faith, it is impossible to please God, because anyone who comes to Him must believe that he exists" (Hebrews 11:6). *God is who he says he is!*

Part 2:

I BELIEVE WHAT HE SAYS HE CAN DO!

"What then shall we say that Abraham, our forefather, discovered in this matter? If, in fact, Abraham was justified by works, he had something to boast about—but not before God. What does the Scripture say? "*Abraham believed God,* and it was credited to him as righteousness." Therefore, the promise comes by faith, so that it may be by grace and may be guaranteed to all Abraham's offspring—not only to those who are of the law but also to those who are of the faith of Abraham. He is the father of us all. As it is written: "I have made you a father of many nations." He is our father in the sight of God, *in whom he believed*—the God who gives life to the dead and calls things that are not as though they were.

Against all hope, Abraham in hope *believed* and so became the father of many nations, just as it

> had been said to him, "So shall your offspring be." Without weakening in his faith, he faced the fact that his body was as good as dead—since he was about a hundred years old—and that Sarah's womb was also dead. Yet he did not waver through unbelief regarding the promise of God, but was strengthened in his faith and gave glory to God, *being fully persuaded that God had power to do what he had promised."*
>
> Romans 4:1–3, 16–21

> "Remember the former things, those of long ago;
> I am God, and there is no other;
>
> I am God, and there is none like me. I make known the end from the beginning, from ancient times, what is still to come. I say: My purpose will stand, and I will do all that I please. From the east I summon a bird of prey; from a far-off land, a man to fulfill my purpose. *What I have said, that will I bring about; what I have planned, that will I do."*
>
> Isaiah 46:9–11

The second part of this has—for some reason—become the hardest part for us as Christians to swallow. We can really get our minds and hearts—our thinking and our emotions—around the fact that *God is who he says he is,* but, we have a harder time with *God can do what he says he can do.* Oh, it was easy for the Israelites, because they saw the plagues, they saw the death angel pass over those who had the blood on their door-frames, and they saw God part the Red

Sea and provide for their needs. When Jesus was here, they saw the lame walk again and the blind see and the dead raised again to life! But that was then, and God doesn't do those things anymore. So it becomes a matter of we don't believe because God doesn't do that, or is it God doesn't do that, because we don't believe?

Beth Moore says in her book, *Believing God,* "We run out of ink in our highlighters marking scriptures that rarely leave the page and hit the pavement!"[11] How true! In the book of Hebrews 3:19, it speaks of the Israelites and says, "So we see that they were not able to enter, (the promised land) *because of their unbelief.*" It wasn't because they didn't know God; it wasn't because they disobeyed God; it was because of their *unbelief!* They didn't believe God could do what he said he could do! So they spent forty years wandering in the desert sand, while all the time blessings and miracles lay just across the river.

In her book, Beth Moore also speaks of how in our society today we have become well acquainted with the term *bipolar disorder.* Perhaps the church could be diagnosed with spiritual bipolar disorder. She suggests that we have been subject to two opposed teachings on both ends of the spectrum concerning what God can do, especially on the subject of faith and miracles. On one extreme, we have what is called *cessationism* and on the other, *sensationalism.* "It seems," she says, "as though Christians find great security in 'always' and 'never'—our 'bipolar' existence."[12]

Cessationism teaches that miracles have ceased in our day, at least the more dramatic "sight-to-the-blind/raising-of-the-dead" kind. Sensationalism teaches that the whole point of faith and belief in God *is* miracles. The tendency is for Christians to be drawn to one extreme or the other. However, there is only one source of truth, and that is God's own Word. If you read Luke 9:41, you will hear Jesus say to those who lack the faith to believe what God can do: "O unbelieving and perverse generation ... how long shall I put up with you?" On the other hand, in Matthew 16:4, to those who demanded a miracle, Jesus says "A wicked and adulterous generation looks for a miraculous sign." I would agree with Beth Moore that both extremes are offensive to God. "Sensationalism prioritizes what God can do and has a tendency to be man-centered," she says, "seeing and depicting God as one big 'miracle machine.' While the other extreme of cessationism, which says 'God doesn't do miracles today,' cheats believers of the real joy of exercising faith and severely undercuts hope." Think about it. If God can't do what he says he can do or if he just doesn't do it any more, then where is our hope? Why do we pray? If we pray just to sound good or to look good, we are to be pitied.

Like Beth Moore, I have to admit that the church as a whole sees only a fraction of what is described in the Gospels and Acts. But, if you haven't figured it out by now, I also believe there is a reason why. Sometimes, the things that God did or the things that Jesus did were for the purpose of proving that God is, and that Jesus was who he said he was! However, in the gospels, Jesus also performed miracles out of compassion. And there were simply times, such as Luke 5:17, "One day as He was teaching, Pharisees and teachers of the law, who had come from every village of Galilee and from Judea and Jerusalem, were sitting there, *and the power of the Lord was present* for Him to heal." The time was right, and it was his will.

One of the problems that I have with sensationalist teaching is the "miracle-on-demand" practice, as if we somehow know and control God. While I surely believe that God can do what he says he can do, I don't think he does it on our command!

That being said, I do think we are a dreadfully unbelieving generation. It is especially true of those of us here in America. Yet reports of miracles and God's power come out of many third world countries, because all they have is their faith. Maybe God is just waiting for us to muster up some real faith and start believing him for who he is and that he can do what he says he can do!

We certainly are not the first generation in this situation. Listen to what happened in Gideon's generation: "When the angel of the Lord appeared to Gideon, he said, "The Lord is with you, mighty warrior." "But sir," Gideon replied, "If the Lord is with us, why has all this happened to us? Where are all His wonders that our fathers told us about?" (Judges 6:12–13).

The rest is history, as they say. God took the thirty-two thousand men that Gideon had and narrowed them down by several different means of elimination to three hundred. With such a small army as this, God defeated the Midianites and the Amalekites of whom it says "were as thick as locusts." What do you think God could do with one church that really believed that God can do what he says he can do today?

Because of who He is, God has proven over and over in his Word that he can do what he says he can do! In Matthew 21:18–22, it says:

> "Early in the morning, as He was on his way back to the city, He was hungry. Seeing a fig tree by the road, He went up to it and found nothing but leaves. Then He said to it, "May you never bear fruit again!" Immediately the tree withered. When the Disciples saw this, they were amazed. "How did the fig tree wither so quickly?" they asked. Jesus replied, "I tell you the truth, if you have faith and do not doubt, not only can you do what was done to the fig tree, but also you can say to this mountain, "Go throw yourself into the sea" and it will be done. If you believe, you will receive whatever you ask for in prayer."

In this sense, if you truly believe, there is no limit on what you may receive! "But when he asks, he must believe and not doubt, because he who doubts is like a wave of the sea, blown and tossed by the wind" (James 1:6).

How often do we pray for something while deep down inside or way in the back of our minds, we don't really think God will do it? That's doubt. Not that we don't believe God is able to do it, but for whatever reason he won't. Maybe it is because we have been brought up closer to the "cessationist" group, the "things-like-that-don't-happen-anymore" group, than we like to think. Listen, if we believe he is able, we must also believe he will!

Do you remember the statement I gave, "A faith

unchallenged is a faith unchanged?" For some people, their faith and their belief system hasn't changed in so long, they have spiritual cobwebs. Galatians 5:25 says, "Since we live by the Spirit, let us keep in step with the Spirit." What does that mean? It means that we need to keep up with what the Spirit is doing culturally and generationally in and through the church. For some, it means that we need to broaden our biblical concepts of who God is and what he can do.

We tend to have a "cut and paste" theology based mostly on denominational views, and the danger in that is the tendency to think that those who are outside of our doctrinal views are somehow wrong or weird in the way they believe and act. I honestly believe God doesn't like extremes either, but that does not mean he is not present or does not work in those churches.

I am simply trying to broaden and strengthen our faith through these statements without packaging our faith in neat, little boxes. We may think we have God in those boxes, but we don't! No matter how many PhDs or LMNOPs someone has after their name or how intelligently and lovely the box is decorated, God doesn't fit. Listen again to God's own words: "For my thoughts are not your thoughts; neither are your ways my ways, declares the Lord. As the heavens are higher than the earth, so are my ways higher than your ways and my thoughts higher than your thoughts" (Isaiah 55:8). "No eye has seen, no ear has heard, no mind has conceived what God has prepared for those who love him" (1 Corinthians 2:9). "To him who is able to do, exceedingly more than we could ever think or imagine" (Ephesians 3:20).

Again, the scripture at the beginning of this part tells us that "Abraham *believed* God, and it was credited to him as righteousness" (Romans 4:3). And he was "*fully persuaded* that God had power to do what he had promised" (Romans 4:21).

It's easy for us to say "Well, I believe all these things," but believing God is not just a statement, it needs to become a lifestyle. And I include myself when I say that most of the time we have a *strong stand* but a *weak walk!* We need to narrow the gap between our stand and our walk by allowing our faith and our experiences to come together to help us believe.

In 2 Corinthians 13:5, Paul says, "Examine yourselves to see whether you are in the faith; test yourselves." This was simply an exercise to stimulate our thinking and help us to know what we believe as well as identify areas where we may be weak in our faith.

Do you believe there are aliens on Mars? Why or why not? We have absolutely no evidence whatsoever. If there were some kind of evidence, would you be more inclined to believe, even if you haven't seen with your own eyes?

Do we have any evidence that God is who he says he is? Of course we do. His Word backs up his creation, and his creation backs up his Word! Is there any evidence that God can do what he says he can do? Of course, we have prophecy. Every prophecy in the Bible has been fulfilled, with the exception of the coming of Jesus Christ!

Although our time is not necessarily characterized by signs and wonders, does God still do miracles? Of course he does. Miracles happen every day all around us. In fact, the Bible says that signs and wonders will actually increase in the latter days. "For false Christs and false prophets will appear and perform great signs and miracles to deceive even the elect—if that were possible" (Matthew 24:24). "The coming of the lawless one will be in accordance with the work of Satan displayed in all kinds of counterfeit miracles signs and wonders, and in every sort of evil that deceives those who are perishing. They perish because they refused to love the truth and so be saved" (2 Thessalonians 2:9).

Though God makes countless exceptions, he still responds most readily to faith. Much of the body of Christ is paralyzed by unbelief. It is a disabling cycle. We see little because we believe little, and we believe little because we see little. God is never offended by our requests for supernatural intervention. He is offended, however, when the desire for signs and wonders eclipses our desire for him or becomes a desire for God to prove himself in some way.

We must choose to believe God and his Word over our own eyes and ears. We need to feel the wind of the Spirit, while standing on the steadfast rock of truth. Psalm 14:2 tells us, "The Lord looks down from heaven on the sons of men to see if there are any who understand, any who seek God." Luke 18:8 asks, "When the Son of Man comes, will he find faith on the earth?"

Probably one of the easiest segues I can make is this next one: It is our belief that God is who he says he is, and our belief that God can do what he says he can do or not do, that make us who and what we are spiritually. This in turn reflects or affects who and what we are naturally.

I choose to believe that I am who God says I am!

Part 3:

I BELIEVE I AM WHO GOD SAYS I AM

A Different Part to Play

The animals decided to get together to organize a school. They developed a curriculum of

climbing, swimming, running, and flying. All animals were required to take all the subjects.

The duck was excellent in swimming, in fact better than the instructor. But the duck's grades in flying were only average. Duck's running grade was very low, because she was so slow. Since duck was so slow, she had to drop swimming—which she really enjoyed—to spend extra time running. Running caused duck's webbed feet to be badly worn so that by the end of the semester duck was only an average swimmer.

The rabbit was at the top of the class in running. Swimming, however, was a challenge for rabbit. Forced to stay after class to improve his swimming technique, rabbit developed a nervous twitch in his leg muscles. Rabbit's speed fell off because of this nasty muscle twitch dropping his running grade from an *A* to a *C*.

The squirrel was excellent in climbing but always had trouble in flying class. The teacher insisted that squirrel start on the ground and go up, but squirrel wanted to start in the treetops and fly down. Squirrel developed cramps in his legs from overexertion, and his grade fell in climbing—which he enjoyed—to a *C+*. His flying teacher gave him a *D*, because he could not follow instructions.

The eagle was always being disciplined. For instance, in flying class, eagle refused to meet his quota in wing flapping, because he preferred to soar. In climbing class eagle beat everyone to the top of the tree, but he insisted on getting there his own way—flying. In swimming class eagle refused to stay in the water; he would dive in but then immediately fly away. And in running class, eagle appeared to outrun the class; the teacher discover eagle had been cheating, because eagle's feet never really touched the ground as he "ran" around the track. Because of eagle's misconduct at animal school, he was suspended for the rest of the school year.

What is the moral of the story? Each animal has its own natural abilities. The animals failed when forced to do something they were not gifted to do. Rabbits don't fly. Eagles don't swim. Squirrels don't have feathers. Ducks look funny trying to climb trees.[13]

What is true of the animals of the forest is also true for you and me. God has not made us all the same. Together we should discover our natural God given abilities and use them in the place God has given us to do it.

I want you to think about something for just a minute; think about the fact that at the point of conception a single egg and a single sperm come together to form a single cell. That single cell contains absolutely everything that makes you who you are—*you!* That single cell contains the forty-six chromosomes—the DNA that is you. You were "fearfully and wonderfully made!" You were—and are—one of God's miracles!

Ladies, you will never be, nor were you meant to be, Raquel Welch or Britney Spears! You were formed to be *you!* I am not, nor was I ever meant to be, Elvis or Billy Graham, God formed me to be *me!* So when we come to grips with that wonderful fact, that I am who God says I am and made me to be, we can stop trying to be like everybody else! We can stop trying to please everyone else. We can stop trying to remake ourselves into the image of what the world describes as perfection and realize that we are already perfect! Look in the mirror and say to yourself; "I'm perfect just the way I am, because God made me, and I am who God says I am!"

> "Praise be to the God and Father of our Lord Jesus Christ, who has blessed us in the heavenly realms with every spiritual blessing in Christ. For he chose us in him before the creation of the world to be holy and blameless in his sight. In love he predestined us to be adopted as his sons through Jesus Christ, in accordance with his pleasure and will—to the praise of his glorious

> grace, which he has freely given us in the One he loves. In him we have redemption through his blood, the forgiveness of sins, in accordance with the riches of God's grace that he lavished on us with all wisdom and understanding. And he made known to us the mystery of his will according to his good pleasure, which he purposed in Christ, to be put into effect when the times will have reached their fulfillment—to bring all things in heaven and on earth together under one head, even Christ."
>
> Ephesians 1:3–10

In preparation for this part, here are a few more scriptures where God describes *who we are.* The first one is of great importance: "Before I formed you in the womb I knew you, before you were born I set you apart" (Jeremiah 1:5).

David gives us the same basic message:

> "For you Created my inmost being; you knit me together in my mother's womb. I praise you because I am fearfully and wonderfully made; your works are wonderful, I know that full well. My frame was not hidden from you when I was made in the secret place. When I was woven together in the depths of the earth, your eyes saw my un-formed body. All the days ordained for me were written in your book before one of them came to be."
>
> Psalm 139:13–16

In this portion of scripture from Ephesians 1, there are six different ways that God describes who we are and what we are *in* him. It says, we are "blessed," we are "chosen," we are "adopted," we are "favored," we are "redeemed," and we are "forgiven." That is worth repeating; we are blessed, chosen, adopted, favored, redeemed, and forgiven! If we knew nothing else the Bible has to say about us but these six things, it ought to be enough to change how we see ourselves. The reason is if these things are true, and they are, then I must be of great worth to God. I must be very valuable to God. Just think about those six words for a moment. It's because we are chosen, adopted, favored, redeemed, and forgiven, we are truly blessed!

We think of *blessed* in terms of receiving physical, tangible things, not just money or possessions, but also loving and being loved, and many of us view our families and friends as a blessing. We also view our health as a blessing. But these are all physical, tangible, here and now blessings. As wonderful as those things are—and we should never take them for granted—the things I listed from this scripture are *for now* and they are *forever!* They are eternal blessings because we are *in* Christ.

How we see ourselves and how we value ourselves is called *self-esteem,* and this is going to be our key word for this part. I spoke of the two extreme views of the church concerning what God can do—one being cessationism and the other sensationalism—with people and denominations in both camps. But there can be extremes in just about everything, including self-esteem. There are those who think they have little or no value or worth, and their self-esteem is at the very low extreme. While there are others who think they are greater, more wonderful, and worth more than they are at the other extreme. It's when we find and believe who and what God says we are that we find balance, stability, security, value, and true worth for our lives.

To take that a step further, what we believe we are affects how we think and act. If you think you are worth nothing and have little or no talent, and if you think you are unloved or unlovely, you will act accordingly. On the other hand, if you think you are greater than you are, you will also act accordingly. We all know someone in both camps, don't we?

Being a child of God, in fact just knowing who we are according to this one scripture, ought to help us think and act differently. This is why the Apostle Paul in the book of Ephesians and in the book of Colossians continued to remind the early church about who they "once were" in the "life you used to live" and how they ought to be thinking and acting now that they had Christ as their Savior and God as their Father! "If you belong to Christ," said Paul, "then you are Abraham's seed, and heirs according to the promise" (Galatians 3:29).

Self-esteem, as the world sees it, always seems to be tied to our abilities and appearance. The American culture places extreme value on these things. We value youth, beauty, athletic ability, intelligence, education, wealth, and fame. But what happens when you have it all and lose it? What happens when Superman becomes a man in a wheelchair? What happens when a supermodel gains some super weight or gets super old? What happens when a super intelligent person has a stroke or gets Alzheimer's? What happens when a superstar ends up in jail or addicted to drugs? What happens when you have a super career, your self-esteem is based on your job, and you lose it? What then? Where do you get your feelings of esteem and personal worth when everything, on which you have based your value, has vanished? This is why we need to believe we are who God says we are and base our self-esteem and our worth on that!

The world wants to single us out according to things which all fall somewhere under "ability" or "appearance." God desires that we work together as a team and as members of one body, different parts with different abilities and gifts, but all working together in harmony!

In the book of Jeremiah, God says to Jeremiah; "Before I formed you in the womb I knew you, before you were born I set you apart" (Jeremiah 1:5). To this, Jeremiah says, "Ah, Sovereign Lord, I'm only a child" (Jeremiah 1:6b). Listen, an accurate view of yourself comes from an understanding of God's view of who you are. If your feelings of self-worth are based on how you see yourself or how others see you, then you are hooked to the wrong star.

Do you know that inferiority is just as bad as being an egotist? It's just another form of pride. One is feeling bad that you are not as good as others, and the other is feeling good that you're not as bad as others!

Pride is a matter of being self-focused. A person who feels constantly inferior is merely someone who is focused upon themselves. They have just as much *I* trouble as the egotist. But as we grow in God, we need to turn the focus away from ourselves and focus upon who and what God says we are.

Don't worry about what you can't do; concentrate on what you can do. Don't worry about whether it is as good as someone else can do it; do the best you can do. What if only the very best tennis player would enter the contest? What if only the best preachers preached? What if only the best singer sang? What if only the wealthiest person gave? What if only the best teacher taught? The truth is, you don't have to be the best, you just have to give your best!

We are to be full of confidence, because God has made us and has called us to serve him. There is no one else like you in the world—God has seen to that. No one else has your particular personality and gifts. You look the way you do, because that is the way he wanted you to look. You have exactly the amount of potential intelligence and ability as he planned for you to have.

There will always be someone with more than you have, there will always be someone with less, but there will never be anyone exactly like you. You are his gift to the world exactly as you are. You can throw down his gifts to you and not use them, or you can pick up those abilities, use them, and develop them to the fullest! You can try to live in your own strength, or you can lean upon his strength; for it is he that has given you the ability and the appearance that you have, and it is he who will enable you to fully develop what he has given you.

What I am trying to say is this: One day your looks will change. Your abilities will diminish. You will not be able to think or remember as you once did … where was I . . . you may lose your friends or even lose your spouse. What then? On what will you base your self-esteem? If your self-esteem is based on your looks, intelligence, education, youth, or abilities, then your self-esteem will be shattered. The only thing that will last—the only thing that no one can take from you and you can never lose—is your relationship with God and your value to him.

All our feelings about ourselves, about others, and life must come from him, or we will live in disillusionment and despair. This relationship with God as your heavenly Father, Jesus Christ as your Savior, and the Holy Spirit as your guide will sustain you and give you a healthy self-esteem. It will provide you with the meaning, fulfillment, and sense of usefulness in life that only God can give.

The story is told of an American tourist in Paris who picked up an amber necklace in a trinket shop. When he arrived at New York and went through customs, he was shocked at the high duty he had to pay. When he came home, he had the necklace appraised, and the jeweler told him he would give $25,000 for the necklace. He was stunned and suspected that there was a reason for the offer. He took the necklace to an expert who appraised it at an astronomical amount. When he asked the appraiser what made the necklace so valuable, he told him to look into the magnifying glass and see for himself. When he placed his eye next to the glass, he saw an inscription which read: "From Napoleon Bonaparte to Josephine." It was the name on the necklace that gave it extraordinary worth.[14]

Inscribed on your life is the name of your owner. He has made you with his own hands and written his name across your life. Your value is found in that inscription. You belong to him, and he wants to use your life. He has made you, and you are his. You are unique. You are very special, because you are special to him. No one else can take your place in his heart. And neither can anyone else take your place in this world. I believe I am who God says I am!

Part 4:

I BELIEVE I CAN DO ALL THINGS THROUGH CHRIST JESUS

"I can do everything through him who gives me strength."

Philippians 4:13

"But he said to me, "My grace is sufficient for you, for my power is made perfect in weakness." That is why, for Christ's sake, I delight in weaknesses, in insults, in hardships, in persecutions, in difficulties, for when I am weak, then I am strong!"

2 Corinthians 12:9a, 10

Do you remember the story called *The Little Engine that Could?* The plot is a bit fuzzy to me now, but the climax of the story is when the little train pulls its oversized load to the top of the hill, finding strength to keep going by repeating the words, "I think I can;

I think I can; I think I can." The moral of the story, being that because it thought positive thoughts, it accomplished the impossible. There is also the *Fraidy Cat* story. It is about a kitten that was frightened by every little thing. Its mother took it to the wise, old owl who presented it with a paper cut-out, which he called the *courage heart.* Wa-la! No more fraidy cat. It's a *Wizard of Oz* kind of thing.

Motivational speakers abound for both youth and adults, enthusiastically reminding us that it's all in the mind. If you think you can do it, then surely you will. This gets brought over into the Christian world by use of this memory verse: "I can do all things through Christ who strengthens me." Why is this verse so popular? No doubt that it is because it carries such a positive message. It's a *can-do* message that is very much in line with the optimism of what we know as the American spirit. People of other countries seem to focus on the things they can't do. But we Americans have a *can-do* mindset.

Two American pastors have brought this particular message to our attention: Norman Vincent Peale on the east coast, who preached for many years on the theme of "positive thinking," and on the west coast, Robert Schuller, founder and pastor of the Crystal Cathedral who promoted a similar idea of "possibility thinking."

Norman Vincent Peale is the name most associated with the idea of positive thinking. Born just prior to the beginning of the 20th century in a rural Ohio town, he grew up helping support his family by delivering newspapers, working in a grocery store, and selling pots and pans door to door. He was a reporter on the Findlay, Ohio, *Morning Republic,* prior to entering the ministry. At age thirty-four, Peale accepted a call to Marble Collegiate Church in Manhattan where he remained for fifty-two years and where he became one of the most popular and influential preachers of the twentieth century. While there, his church grew from four hundred to over five thousand. His list of accomplishments is impressive. However, no doubt his best known accomplishment was the famous book, *The Power of Positive Thinking.* Published in 1952, it has sold millions of copies in forty-one languages. To a certain extent, I also believe in the power of positive thinking. I believe a healthy, positive mental attitude is beneficial in all things. I think most people would have to agree.

So is this the same thing Paul is trying to get across when he writes, "I can do all things through Christ who gives me strength?" I believe there is a subtle difference. It's not just right thinking. It's not just mind over matter like that repeated by the little train; "I think I can; I think I can." Paul's message is very clear, it is through Christ—having and knowing the power of Christ in my life—that what was thought to be impossible now becomes possible. But note this: if it is *in Christ,* it will be consistent with the character and purposes of Christ. Let me repeat that: if it is *in Christ,* it will be consistent with the *character* and *purposes* of Christ.

What I think is important to point out is that in this verse, there is a balance; there is a partnership. There is the *I can do,* and there is the *through Christ.* I have a part to play in meeting the challenges, I have a part to play when facing the difficulties and overcoming the temptations, and I certainly have a part to play in living up to the high standard of holiness imposed by God's Word. Thankfully, I have a partner so that I am able to say, "I can do all things through Christ." But depending on his strength does not allow me to abdicate my responsibility or my effort. Some people emphasize one part, the *I can*—like Peale and Schuller. Other people emphasize the *through Christ* part, operating with the notion that God does it all, and there's nothing they need to do.

It's easy to use the excuses. "God's still working on me" or "God isn't finished with me yet," putting the emphasis on God's part of the transforming process. When at the same time, we aren't doing anything! We are not putting forth the effort to grow and change. It's a partnership! I am the instrument; he is the power. I have the ability through him who provides the ability! Without him, I am nothing.

So then, is this a message on positive thinking? No, it's a positive message from God and his Word. "I can do all things through Christ who strengthens me." However, we must take this verse in the context of the whole of what Paul is talking about. It is apparent that the message has to do with endurance. He just finished saying, "I can make it through poverty or plenty," as if to say I can handle it all. "I can make it through when I have nothing," "I can make it through when there is abundance," and "I can make it with the power that Christ offers."

Secondly, it has to do with overcoming temptation. You see, those who are in poverty are tempted to covet, steal, or cheat to get ahead. On the other hand, those who live with abundance have to fight the temptation to spend and depend on their money. Neither one is a healthy attitude for Christians to have.

Attitude is what it is all about, a healthy, positive attitude about God, about Christ, about the church, and especially about life. When Jesus started his ministry, the first thing he did was to set the people down on a hillside and teach them about the Beattitudes. He had to teach them to change the way they thought. He had to help them change their attitudes about life issues. The book of Matthew, chapters five, six, and seven are all devoted to this teaching. Then, Jesus follows this up with "seek first the kingdom of God," and everything else will fall into place.

(my paraphrase)!

When we get saved, we're not left to be on our own; he says, "I am with you always, even to the end of the age." He gives us the strength to do what he's called us to do. I can do all things is a kind of self-sufficient thing to say but only when used without the rest of the verse.

Paul has many companion verses to this.

- "Not that we are competent in ourselves, but our competence comes from God. He has made us competent as ministers of the new covenant" (2 Corinthians 3:5).
- "I have been crucified with Christ: and I no longer live, but Christ lives in me" (Galatians 2:20).

- "I know what it is to be in need, and I know what it is to have plenty. I have learned the secret of being content in any and every situation, whether well fed or hungry, whether living in plenty or in want. I can do everything through him who gives me strength" (Philippians 4:12, 13).

In Philippians, Paul is echoing the teaching of Jesus when Jesus said in John 15:5, "I am the vine; you are the branches. If a man remains in me and I in him, he will bear much fruit; apart from me you can do nothing." It doesn't get much clearer, does it? On the one hand, we're told that apart from Christ, we can do nothing of lasting value in our lives. On the other, we're told that we can do everything through Christ who gives us strength. One of those *everythings* is found in the context of this scripture; which is finding contentment in all situations. But it also goes beyond just contentment to include overcoming fear, discouragement, and "impossibility thinking."

Here's the truth: whether you are experiencing plenty or want in your life right now, the secret to being content—to finding peace—is staying connected to Jesus. It is his strength that will provide the contentment you need. It is his power that will help you overcome the fears in life. And it is his presence that will keep us from being discouraged. It is also in him that we have hope, even when the cupboards are bare or the prognosis is not good. It is in and through Christ that we overcome the darts of discouragement, disbelief, and doubt, which Satan throws our way.

When we are spending time on a regular basis praying, studying God's word, and surrendering our lives to the power of the Holy Spirit, we are going to find that no matter what else is going on in our life, no matter what the situation or circumstance, we will feel more content and more at peace with it all.

If there was anyone who could feel discontentment and be discouraged about his life and the situations surrounding his life, it was Paul. Here was a man who was beaten, shipwrecked, imprisoned, ridiculed, nearly stoned to death, and mocked by his peers, and yet he says he has found the secret to being content, being at peace in all things! Some of us get a hangnail and think it's the end of the world!

Listen to some of the things God has to say in his Word about those who are in Christ and who stand on and believe this principle:

- "And my God will meet all your needs according to his glorious riches in Christ Jesus" (Philippians 4:19).
- "And God is able to make all grace abound to you, so that in all things at all times, having all that you need, you will abound in every good work" (2 Corinthians 9:8).

Paul realizes that he himself is weak. If he relied on his own thinking, his own understanding, and his own power, he could not and would not endure anything! Neither will we. "But," he said, "I have come to know and believe that I can do all things through Christ, who gives me strength," even in the face of death, and Paul certainly faced death many times in his life.

You see, (and this is worth highlighting) our potential as Christians—our potential as a church—is only limited by what we believe we cannot do! A man named Paul Hovey once said, "A blind man's world is bound by the limits of his touch; an ignorant man's world is bound by the limits of his knowledge; a great man's world is bound by the limits of his vision." If our vision is limited to only this world—what we can see, feel, touch, hear, or smell—then we will be limited to that vision. And we will never go beyond its boundaries. It's only when we begin to see and believe in the eternal realm—in, around, above, and beyond this world—that we begin to expand the boundaries of our thinking and our potential. In other words, we need to believe that God is, that God can do, and that I am who he says I am; and that I can do all things with God by my side and Jesus Christ in my life! Amen!

I think of the story in the Bible of Peter walking on the water. Now picture this: the storm is raging, the wind is blowing, the waves are coming up over the sides of the boat, and Peter and the disciples are in the middle of a storm. Sometimes we are in the middle of an emotional or spiritual or even physical storm that is frightening. The circumstances seem difficult to overcome. We are afraid to take a risk and get out of the boat for fear that we will drown!

In the story, they saw from a distance a man walking on the water. They were afraid. And Jesus said, "It is I, do not be afraid." And while the other disciples are bailing for all they are worth, Peter does something amazing! He expands the boundaries of his thinking, he expands the limits of his faith and his potential, and he says, "Lord, if it is you, bid me come!"

Now why didn't he just wait for Jesus to get to the boat and calm the storm? I think Peter saw with his heart, his mind, and his spirit that there was something beyond the physical. He saw that Jesus had power, which could not be limited to the physical, it overcame his fear and his discouragement, and he stepped out of the boat! *Our potential is only limited by what we believe we cannot do, because we don't really believe what God can do.*

Every Christian can and must reach the point of making this same statement of faith: I can do all things—I can find contentment and peace in all things, I can overcome my fears and have courage in all things—through Christ who strengthens me. I can be the person that he has called me to be. I can be a godly Christian father. I can be the husband that God wants me to be. We can make this marriage, the marriage that God would have it to be! We can face the pressures that come our way. I can overcome this habit. I can defeat this giant in my life. I can accomplish whatever God calls me to do *through Christ who strengthens me!*

The reason that David wasn't afraid to face Goliath—no matter how big or powerful he was—is because David knew four things that Goliath didn't know! The reason Daniel could sleep with the lions was because he knew four things that King Darius didn't know. The reason Shadrack, Meshack, and Abednego didn't burn in the furnace was because they knew four things that King Nebuchadnezzar didn't know. Are you getting the picture? All things may seem impossible, unless you know and believe that (1) God is who he says he is, (2) God can do what he says he can do, (3) I am who and what God says I am, and (4) I can do all things through Christ who strengthens me! We need to remind ourselves often of the Lord's promise to "make a way when there seems to be no way."

God gave Joshua some promises that would assure victory. Let's look at the words once again. God says in Joshua 1:3, 5: "I will give you every place where you set your foot ... No one will be able to stand up to you all the days of your life. As I was with Moses, so I will be with you; I will never leave you nor forsake you!" Wouldn't you take some steps of faith, if God said those things to you? Well, he does!

God did not want Joshua to fall for the two most effective deterrents to our faith: fear and discouragement. So, four times in just four verses, he tells Joshua, "Be strong and courageous." In verse nine, once again, he says, "Do not be afraid; do not be discouraged; for the Lord your God will be with you wherever you go." Fear and discouragement can paralyze even the best of us.

Remember this, *"Faith is never the denial of reality ... it is belief in a greater reality!"* (Beth Moore–*Believing God* pg.113) The truth is that we are surrounded by terrifying and discouraging circumstances. The disciples were in the midst of a storm! Daniel was in a pit of lions! The fire in the furnace was extremely hot! What makes the difference is the presence of the Lord: "As I was with Moses, so I will be with you," "I will never leave you nor forsake you," "Lo, I am with you always," "With God, all things are possible," and

"I can do all things through Christ who strengthens me!" If you believe it, say a hearty *Amen!*

This isn't just a feel good memory verse; it is sound theology that needs to become reality.

> I believe that God is who he says he is !
>
> I believe that God can do what he says he can do !
>
> I believe that I am who God says I am !
>
> I believe that I can do all things through Christ Jesus ![15]

Grow:

GETTING TO KNOW GOD BETTER

"And we pray this in order that you may live a life worthy of the Lord and may please him in every way: bearing fruit in every good work, growing in the knowledge of God."

Colossians 1:10

Part 1

OUR KNOWLEDGE OF HIM

"To those who through the righteousness of our God and Savior Jesus Christ have received a faith as precious as ours: Grace and peace be yours in abundance through the *knowledge* of God and of Jesus our Lord. His divine power has given us everything we need for life and godliness through our *knowledge* of Him who called us by His own glory and goodness. Through these He has given us His very great and precious promises, so that through them you may participate in the divine nature and escape the corruption in the world caused by evil desires.

For this very reason, make every effort to add to your faith goodness; and to goodness, *knowledge;* and to knowledge, self-control; and to self-control, perseverance; and to perseverance, godliness; and to godliness, brotherly kindness; and to brotherly kindness, love. For if you possess these qualities in increasing measure, they will keep you from being ineffective and unproduc-

> tive in your *knowledge* of our Lord Jesus Christ. But if anyone does not have them, he is near-sighted and blind, and has forgotten that he has been cleansed from his past sins.
>
> Therefore, my brothers, be all the more eager to make your calling and election sure. For if you do these things, you will never fall, and you will receive a rich welcome into the eternal kingdom of our Lord and Savior Jesus Christ. So I will always remind you of these things, even though you know them and are firmly established in the truth you now have." (emphasis mine).
>
> 2 Peter 1:3–12

So, now that I believe God is, and God can do, the question becomes "How do I get to know him better?" Well, let me ask this: Do you consider yourself to be a *theologian?* Maybe this will help: theology is the study of God. So are you a theologian? We tend to think of a theologian as a person who has thoroughly studied the Bible and knows all there is to know about God. However, theology is not a past-tense term; it is a present-tense term. God tells us in his Word that he wants us to know him. He wants us to know all about him. But he especially wants us to know him, because in this, there is great reward.

Listen again to the words of these verses: "His divine power has given us everything we need for life and godliness;" the two most important things we can understand are *life* and *godliness.* They come "through our *knowledge* of him." Note the emphasis on *knowledge:-* "Make every effort to add to your faith". And "if you possess these qualities in *ever-increasing* measure, they will keep you from being ineffective and unproductive in your *knowledge* of Christ"(2 Peter 1:8). 2 Peter 3:18 says, we are to "grow in the grace and *knowledge* of our Lord and Savior." Also in Philippians 1:9, we read "that your love may abound more and more in *knowledge* and depth of insight."

This is not knowledge of everything in the world, but knowledge concerning God and of Christ. It is also not just an intellectual knowledge (knowing about God), but it is a knowledge that comes from a *relationship* and *experiences* that are ever growing, ever increasing, and on-going.

The subject of God is so vast that our thoughts often get lost in its immensity; it is so deep that our finite minds drown in its infinity. The wonderful thing about a study of God is that we tend not to become the wiser but to be humbled. Yet, while it may humble the mind, at the same time it also expands the mind. If we disregard the study of God and knowing God better, we stumble through life "blindfolded" (so to speak) with no sense of direction or understanding of what life is all about. Man basically has three questions that need to be answered: (1) "Where did I come from?" (2) "Why am I here?" (3) "Where am I going?" Our knowledge of God can answer all three.

So, let's get started. There are six basic foundational principles that we have concerning God:

1. God is Creator and Ruler over all things.
   In a word it's called *sovereignty.*

2. God is Savior. Acting in sovereign love, God supplied the only way of salvation through the free gift of salvation through Jesus Christ.
3. God is holy. He is perfect, pure, and *whole.*
4. God is Triune: God the Father, Jesus the Son, and the Holy Spirit. All of whom are active in the believers life.
5. God's desire is for us to live in godliness and to "make every effort," as the Word says, to become Christlike. Not to become God nor to be and do everything Christ did, but to conform to the character or character traits of Christ.
6. God has spoken to man, and God speaks to man.

For most of us, just an exploration of those six themes would give us plenty to ponder and digest. Sometimes we are like a traveler who has surveyed a great mountain from afar. He has traveled all around it. He has observed it from all angles. And now is ready to don the ropes and spikes and to begin climbing the mountain. It is in the climbing, which we get to know what the mountain is really like.

There is a big difference in talking to someone who has seen Mount Everest and someone who has climbed Mount Everest. Just like there is a difference between someone who knows all about God and someone who knows God. Most of the Israelites knew about God, had seen his glory, and witnessed his miracles, but Moses *knew* God! "This is eternal life; that they may know you, the only true God, and Jesus whom you have sent" (John 17:3). In this chapter we shall explore the possibilities of knowing God even more than we do now.

In the book of Jeremiah 9:23, it reads,

> "This is what the Lord says; Let not the wise man boast of his wisdom; or the strong man boast of his strength; or the rich man boast of his riches; but let him who boasts boast about this; that he *understands* and *knows* me."

When someone knows God and has a relationship with him, there are evidences of it in their lives.

Those who know God shall "stand firm and take action," says Daniel 11:32. In a world of ungodliness and apostasy, they stand firm in their faith and take action against those things that dishonor God. Such is the story of Daniel and his three friends in the book of Daniel chapter three.

Those who know God desire to spend as much time as possible with him. Whether in worship, study, prayer, or devotions—all these become priorities in our life. Remember, our desire is to know him better. When I first met my wife Judy, I wanted to spend as much time as possible with her! I wanted to know her better.

Those who know God have boldness for God. They are neither afraid nor ashamed of their faith or their testimony of what God has done in their lives. Their boldness is not "arrogance," which pushes people away, but rather it draws others to want to know this God too. Remember, you can only testify to that which you have experienced personally. You cannot live the Christian life on hearsay.

Those who know God know peace: peace of mind, peace of heart, and peace of soul. They have peace with God. And with peace comes contentment.

These are the things that cause us to remember verses like:

- "There is now no condemnation for those who are in Christ Jesus" (Romans 8:1).
- "We know that in all things God works for the good of those who love Him" (Romans 8:28).
- "If God is for us, who can be against us" (Romans 8:31).
- "Who shall separate us from the love of Christ?" (Romans 8:35).
- "It is He who supplies seed to the sower" (2 Corinthians 9:10).
- Yes, he has truly "given us everything we need for life and godliness, through our knowledge of him" (2 Peter 1:3).

"The heavens declare the glory of God; the skies proclaim the work of His hands. Day after day they pour forth speech; night after night they display knowledge. There is no speech or language where their voice is not heard. Their voice goes out into all the earth, their words to the ends of the world. In the heavens He has pitched a tent for the sun, which is like a bridegroom coming forth from his pavilion, like a champion rejoicing to run his course. It rises at one end of the heavens and makes its circuit to the other; nothing is hidden from its heat. The law of the Lord is perfect, reviving the soul. The statutes of the Lord are trustworthy, making wise the simple. The precepts of the Lord are right, giving joy to the heart. The commands of the Lord are radiant, giving light to the eyes. The fear of the Lord is pure, enduring forever. The ordinances of the Lord are sure and altogether righteous. They are more precious than gold, than much pure gold; they are sweeter than honey, than honey from the comb. By them is your servant warned; in keeping them there is great reward."

Psalm 19:1–11

When we look at the world in which we live, the vastness of the heavens, as well as the beauty of a delicate flower, it immediately spawns the questions: Who? What? When? Where? Why? How? In searching for answers to those questions man has two avenues to pursue. One leads to God, the other away from God. One accepts "In the beginning, God," the other does not. The Bible matter-of-factly states that "anyone who comes to him must believe he exists"

(Hebrews 11:6). That's step one. We cannot search in the direction of God without step one.

We can get to know God better, because God has chosen to reveal himself in three specific ways: (1)

through his Creation, (2) through his Spirit, and (3) through his Word.

Verses seven through eleven of this scripture speak of God's Word, and we are given five different terms to describe it: his Law, statutes, precepts, commands, and his ordinances. The natures of these terms are described as perfect, trustworthy, right, radiant, pure, sure, and righteous. And the result of knowing these things, it says, revives the soul, gives wisdom, gives joy to the heart, gives light to the eyes, endures forever, and are all together more precious than gold.

One thing we should note is the last thing it says in verse eleven. "By them your servant is warned." What parent has never said to their child, "Don't say I didn't warn you?" But in keeping them, in doing them, and in applying them to our lives, "there is great reward," not just reward in the sweet by and by, but great reward here and now! The avoidance of pain and stress and the consequences of wrong choices is great reward, is it not?

Imagine that we are going to be introduced to someone whom we feel is above us, whether in rank, intellect, professional skill, riches, or some other aspect. Think of meeting the president of the United States. We may want to get to know this person better, but we realize that this really is their decision, not ours. If they confine themselves to courteous formalities, we may be disappointed, but we can't complain, because we have no claim on their friendship. It's enough to just shake their hand.

But what if they decided to take us into their confidence, befriend us, and maybe even ask us to join them in a particular undertaking they have planned? What if they ask us to make ourselves available, because they need us to make it successful? How would it make you feel? I think we would feel privileged. I think it would completely change our outlook on the future. I think we would knuckle down, prepare, and do everything in our power to do whatever is asked of us.

This, of course, is an illustration of what it means to know God. Not only does he want us to work with him in his plan, but he has gifted us and enabled us to make it successful. He desires that we work together with him as a team to make sure it gets done! It has been that way from the very beginning, and ever shall be!

"I am the Alpha and the Omega," says the Lord God, "who is, and who was, and who is to come, the Almighty" (Revelation 1:8). "Behold, I am coming soon! My reward is with me, and I will give to everyone according to what He has done. I am the Alpha and the Omega, the First and the Last, the Beginning and the End" (Revelation 22:12–14).

Our reading of the Bible takes us into a different world, the near eastern world, as it was thousands of years ago. In that world, we meet people like Abraham, Moses, Joshua, David, the prophets, John the Baptist, and of course Jesus. And we can also read about the early beginnings of the church from the book of Acts and on through the epistle letters. It's all very interesting, but it seems so far away, so long ago. How can this have any effect or help those of us who live in the age of technology?

The link between the past, the present, and the future is God! The God of the Bible is the same God of today. I could sharpen that point even more by saying he is *exactly* the same God. God never changes. In Malachi 3:6, we read "I the LORD do not change." This scripture from the book of Revelation tells us that God is the "Alpha and the Omega, the beginning and the end, from everlasting to everlasting, he is God." So, in our pursuit to know God better, let's look at some *changeless factors* concerning God:

First, God himself never changes. Created things have a beginning and an end, but not God. This is one of those mysteries that will put you in the nuthouse, if you try to figure it out rather than just accept it. We cannot ask the question where did God come from, because God always existed, and it was he who created everything else. God will always exist, he has no end because God is eternal, and in eternity, there is no time. That's all we need to know! God does not grow older. He does not get stronger or weaker. He does not gain or lose power. He does not get any wiser over time. He cannot change for the better, because he is already perfect!

In Exodus 3, God told Moses that his name was I AM. God did not say I was or I will be but I AM. So if you ask God, "Were you there in the past?" He would say I AM!

God, himself, never changes. He is the God of Abraham, Isaac, Jacob, and Rev. Fred! Just think about the fact that the same God who parted the Red Sea, went before the Israelites, totally consumed Elijah's offering, healed the sick, gave sight to the blind, and gave boldness and wisdom to the Disciples, the same God who was able to totally and radically transform a man like Saul into the person of Paul is the God who loves us, cares for us, provides for us and whom we love and serve and worship today! He never changes. He is gracious, compassionate, merciful, and forgiving. Yet he is also holy and just. He does not leave the guilty unpunished.

Second, God's character never changes. We are ever-changing creations. We change with circumstances. We change with the weather. We change as we grow and mature. We change our mind as often as we change our socks! But God's character never changes! Let's look to Exodus 34, and read some of the changeless character traits that God told Moses:

> "Then the Lord came down in the cloud and stood there with Him and proclaimed His name, the Lord. And He passed in front of Moses, proclaiming, "The Lord, the Lord, the compassionate and gracious God, slow to anger, abounding in love and faithfulness, maintaining love to thousands, and forgiving wickedness, rebellion and sin. Yet He does not leave the guilty unpunished; *He punishes the children and their children for the sin of the fathers to the third and fourth generation.*"
>
> Exodus 34:5–7

How does that make you feel? Meditate on this for a few moments. It would be a good study idea to keep a list and write down something you learn about God as you read Scripture.

Third, God's Word and his truth never change. When Joshua was to replace Moses as leader of the Israelites, he had been at Moses' side for forty years or more, yet God's command to him was not to try and remember all the things Moses had said and done nor to try and to be like Moses. He told Joshua to search and constantly study and meditate on the Scriptures. We are admonished to do the same today. People change, fashions change, pastors come and go, but the Word of God never changes. God's Word is truth for all generations. However, all generations have to find the knowledge of God themselves—personally!

Fourth, the power of God never changes. God's power was displayed in many ways throughout the Old Testament. His power was displayed in and through Jesus in the Gospels. And his power was displayed through the Holy Spirit in Acts through Revelation and still is displayed today. Is God out of the miracle working business? I don't think so. He certainly has done some in my life! I no longer believe in coincidence.

From us he requires faith, trust, obedience, and a godly attitude. When that is the case, he will keep his promises, and he will provide. God can still do today what he has always done!

Fifth, the purpose of God never changes. Psalm 33:11 tells us, "The plans of the Lord stand firm forever; the purposes of His heart throughout all generations." What God does in time, he planned for eternity, and all that God planned for eternity, he carries out in time.

All that he has committed himself to do in his Word will be done! His purpose for the world, for his Creation, and his purpose for man never changes. "For those God foreknew he predestined to be conformed to the likeness of His Son" (Romans 8:29). From the very beginning, God said, "Let us make man in our image;" his purpose hasn't changed. When man first sinned in the book of Genesis, the image and character of God was tarnished, and the rest of the Bible is all about God trying to restore his image and his character in man.

Let's not lose tract of what this chapter is all about. It is based on Jeremiah 9:23, which says, "Let not the wise man boast of his wisdom, or the strong man boast of his strength, or the rich man of his riches, but let him who boasts boast of this; that he *knows me;* says the Lord Almighty."

One thing I believe is that our view of God has suffered from our failure to capture a sense of his Majesty. The God of contemporary evangelism is a very personal God. He is someone with whom we can enjoy intimate fellowship. He is our best friend and closest ally; the one to whom we can bring all of our troubles. We have a great high priest who became flesh and blood so that he can be a perfect mediator between himself and man. But in stressing our closeness to God in all these ways, I think we have lost sight of his majesty.

Isaiah had opportunity to look beyond the visible to the realms of the invisible and see the majesty of our God. He saw God sitting upon a throne, the symbol of sovereign authority, in charge of everything in heaven and upon the earth. People in countries like older England, which has an impressive tradition of royalty and a reigning king that is accorded the utmost respect and allegiance, have a better understanding of majesty than we do today in the United States. Our leaders are subjected to intense scrutiny, often harsh criticism, and unjustified attacks. We don't get the sense of majesty and respect in the tone of our media as they talk about our leaders. Instead our leaders are the subject of laughter and ridicule as our comedians make a living off of their perceived weaknesses and mistakes. There is something about *majesty,* which commands respect, dignity, and a sense of awe.

The word *majesty,* when ascribed to God, is not only a declaration of his greatness but also an invitation to worship. Upon having his vision of God upon the throne, how long do you think it took Isaiah to hit the floor face down? The word *majesty* also has with it a sense of reverent fear or humbleness on our part. I personally feel that when we stop singing the great old hymns of the church, we also stop seeing and feeling the *majesty* of God. We truly need to be reminded often of the omniscience, omnipotence, and the omnipresence of Almighty God.

> "Who has measured the waters in the hollow of his hand, or with the breadth of Hs hand marked off the heavens? Who has held the dust of the earth in a basket, or weighed the mountains on the scales and the hills in a balance? Who has understood the mind of the LORD, or instructed Him as his counselor? Whom did the LORD consult to enlighten Him, and who taught Him the right way? Who was it that taught him knowledge or showed him the path of understanding? Surely the nations are like a drop in a bucket; they are regarded as dust on the scales; He weighs the islands as though they were fine dust. Lebanon is not sufficient for altar

fires, nor its animals enough for burnt offerings. Before him all the nations are as nothing; they are regarded by Him as worthless and less than nothing. To whom, then, will you compare God? What image will you compare him to? As for an idol, a craftsman casts it, and a goldsmith overlays it with gold and fashions silver chains for it. A man too poor to present such an offering selects wood that will not rot. He looks for a skilled craftsman to set up an idol that will not topple. Do you not know? Have you not heard? Has it not been told you from the beginning? Have you not under-stood since the earth was founded? He sits enthroned above the circle of the earth, and its people are like grasshoppers. He stretches out the heavens like a canopy, and spreads them out like a tent to live in. He brings princes to naught and reduces the rulers of this world to nothing. No sooner are they planted, no sooner are they sown, no sooner do they take root in the ground, than He blows on them and they wither, and a whirlwind sweeps them away like chaff. "To whom will you compare me? Or who is my equal?" says the Holy One. Lift your eyes and look to the heavens: Who created all these? He who brings out the starry host one by one, and calls them each by name. Because of His great power and mighty strength, not one of them is missing. Why do you say, O Jacob, and complain, O Israel, "My way is hidden from the Lord; my cause is disregarded by my God?" Do you not know? Have you not heard? The Lord is the everlasting God, the Creator of the ends of the earth. He will not grow tired or weary, and His understanding no one can fathom. He gives

> strength to the weary and increases the power of the weak. Even youths grow tired and weary, and young men stumble and fall; but those who hope in the LORD will renew their strength. They will soar on wings like eagles; they will run and not grow weary, they will walk and not be faint."
>
> Isaiah 40:12–31

The more knowledge I gain of God and from God, the more words like "Holy, Holy, Holy" and "Worship his Majesty" fill my mind and soul.

Part 2:

UNDERSTANDING WISDOM

In my NIV introduction to the book of Proverbs, it says this.

> The Jews often speak of the Old Testament as the Law, the Prophets, and the Writings. Included within the Writings are the Psalms, Job, Proverbs, and Ecclesiastes. These are also called the *wisdom* books. Whereas the priests and prophets dealt more with the religious side of life, the so-called "wise men," the sages and teachers of the law, dealt with practical and philosophical matters.

So one might say that wisdom is not only to be found in knowledge, but it is also found in common sense—the practical, everyday matters. It has been said that many people are *knowledgeable* but have no common sense. They can quote from the greatest books but can't change a light bulb!

JI Packer, a well-known author, says that "Wisdom is the power to see, and the inclination to choose, the best and highest goal; together with the means of attaining it."[16] As such, wisdom finds its fullness only in God. The reason is because human wisdom can be frustrated by circumstantial factors, which are outside of the wisest person's control. God's wisdom, however, cannot be frustrated, because of its alliance with his omniscient, omnipotent power. Infinite power guided by infinite wisdom; infinite wisdom attainable by infinite power. This is God's character as described in scripture. "His *wisdom* is profound, his *power* is vast" (Job 9:4). "He is mighty in *power* and in *wisdom*" (Job 12:13). "*Wisdom and power* are his" (Daniel 2:20) - "Now, to him that is of *power* to establish you according to my gospel … to the only *wise* God … " (Romans 16:25–27)

Listen, wisdom without power would be pathetic. Power without wisdom is just plain frightening! But, in God, absolute power and absolute wisdom are united, and that makes him worthy of our trust and faith.

We often have the tendency to question God's wisdom when we ask questions like, "How could a God, who is love, allow this to happen?" In effect, we may think we are questioning his motives, but we are really questioning his wisdom. This is because many misunderstand the Bible when it says, "God is Love." They think that, if God is love, then he intends a trouble free life. So anything upsetting, such as accident, illness, or suffering of any kind, indicates that the Bible is wrong or that somehow God's power and wisdom have broken down. But God's wisdom and power is not, and never was, pledged to keep a fallen world happy! Nor is it meant to make ungodliness comfortable! Not even to Christians does God promise a trouble-free life. In fact, his Word tells us just the opposite. Happiness, pure joy, and an absolute trouble-free life is God's reward of heaven not of earth.

When the old theologians dealt with the attributes of God, they used to classify them into two categories: those that were communicable and those that were incommunicable. Many of the incommunicable we have already talked about. Things that show how God is so vastly different from us: his self-existence, the fact that he is never-changing, not limited by space and time, all knowing, all powerful, ever-present, and absolute holiness and perfection, which means that there are, in him, no elements that can conflict. So, unlike us, he cannot be torn in two different directions by thoughts and desires. These are things that man does not share with God, they are found in him alone.

In the *communicable* group, they lumped together qualities like spirituality, goodness, kindness, truth, righteousness, love, and the like. In a word, it's called *godliness* or *Godlikeness.* When the Bible says we were created in God's image, these are the qualities, which we have in common with God. Many of these qualities were lost in the fall of man and man lapsed into *ungodliness.* But God in his infinite wisdom had a plan, a plan of redemption and restoration, a plan to communicate these godly qualities in a new and fresh way. That's what Scripture means when it says we are "being renewed day by day" and "becoming Christlike," which is God's purpose.

Now among these *communicable* attributes, theologians put *wisdom.* As God is wise in himself, so he imparts wisdom to man whom he has created. The first nine chapters of Proverbs are devoted to this subject of wisdom and are worthy of your reading, meditation, and study.

In the New Testament, we are told to "Live as wise, not as unwise" (Ephesians 5:15) and "Be wise in the way you act toward outsiders" (Colossians 4:5). "If any of you lacks wisdom, he should ask God, and it will be given unto him" (James 1:5).

Where can we find the wisdom of God? The Bible tells us that we must first learn to reverence or "fear" God. For it says, "The fear of God is the beginning of *wisdom.*" We must also learn to receive and understand God's Word. Paul wrote to the Colossians, "Let the word of Christ dwell in you richly, as you teach and admonish one another with all *wisdom*" (Colossians 3:16). He also told Timothy that "All scripture is able to make you *wise* for salvation" (2 Timothy 3:15). Many today who profess to be Christians never learn wisdom. I challenge you to look at your own life and ask, "Where does my wisdom come from?" Do you spend as much time in God's Word as you do reading the newspaper or watching TV?

I close this part of our knowing God better with two stories of what wisdom is and what it is not.

If you were to stand on the platform of York Station, you could watch a constant movement of engines and trains, a lot of trains, going this way and that. You might be able to get a rough idea [17]of what's going on, and perhaps an overall plan of these movements. But, suppose you were taken to the main signal room, where there is a whole-wall diagram of the entire railway station. There are little glowworm lights, which mark movement and non-movement of all the trains on all the tracks. You would be able to see the entire pattern and better understand the whys and wherefores of all the movements.

Now the mistake is commonly made to suppose this is an illustration of what God does when he bestows wisdom. That is that wisdom consists of a deepened understanding into the meaning and purpose of the events going on in the world or in an individual's life. However, this is not wisdom.

Wisdom is like being taught to drive. What matters in driving are the speed and the reactions to what is happening around you and the soundness of your judgment in any given situation. You see, you are not worried about why the road twists and turns or where the other cars are going, you simply see and do the right thing in the situation you are in every time you drive.

The effect of divine wisdom enables you and me to do the same thing in everyday life. The wisdom of God is far beyond our comprehension. But the wisdom he imparts to us in his Word gives us the power to see and the "inclination to choose, the best and highest goals ... together with the means that we need to achieve them!"

Part 3:

UNDERSTANDING TRUTH

I want to begin by saying that all the things we have been looking at are not directed to know more about God but an attempt to know God better. The main goal of knowledge is understanding. The goal of understanding is application. In application there is great wisdom and reward.

In this lesson, we are going to focus on the *truth* of God. Let's look at John 17:17, which says, "Sanctify them by the truth; Thy Word is truth." Let's look at that for just a moment. What does the word *sanctify* mean? It simply means to be set apart for God's purpose. For example, in a church there can be many rooms, but the place where we worship God is called the s*anctuary.* As God's people, as Christians, we are called to be set apart. However, the previous verse tells us that it does not mean that we are to be "taken out of the world" or that we should have nothing to do with the world. What it does say is that we can be "protected from the evil one," Satan, the devil, and all his schemes, temptations, and attempts to get our eyes off of God. And how does it say we are to be protected, set apart, or *sanctified?* By the truth. "Thy Word is truth."

Now, we actually have—literally—God's words within his Word. So we can hold up the Bible, God's Word, and say that this is truth. In its entirety and in each and every part of it, it is truth.

Within God's Word, we have God's words that are given to us in various forms or applications. For instance, in the first chapter of Genesis we have the story of creation. Where did this story come from? I believe that while Moses was on the mountain with God for forty days, God shared with him the story that became the first nine chapters of Genesis. This is categorized as *God's creative word.* God said, "Let there be," and it came into being!

Next, the story goes on to a further stage where God speaks to the man and the woman whom he has made, and the fellowship or relationship between them is begun. God's first word to them is a *word of command,* telling them to "Be fruitful, and increase in number; fill the earth and subdue it. Rule over the fish of the sea, and over the birds of the air, and over every living creature that moves on the ground" (Genesis 1:28).

Then comes God's *word of testimony,* in which God explains certain things to Adam and Eve like how he has made all the plants and fruits for them and the animals to eat (man was at first a vegetarian).

Next comes God's *word of prohibition.* God tells them not to eat from the tree of knowledge of good and evil, "for when you eat of it, you shall surely die."

Then, after the fall, comes God's *word of prom-*

ise both favorable and unfavorable. Now the rest of the Bible, of course, is filled with many words from God, but they all fall into one of these five categories of: creative words, words of command, words of testimony, words of prohibition, and words of promise. We are called to believe and obey God's Word, not just because he tells us to, but because it is truth! No matter which category it falls in to.

Truth is God's nature, and he doesn't have anything in him to be anything else. His truth shows us the way things really are and how things will be in the future, whether or not we choose to believe or heed his words.

The book of Titus begins with the words, "Paul, a servant of God and an Apostle of Jesus Christ, for the faith of God's elect and the *knowledge of truth* that leads to godliness" (Titus 1:1). Whether physical, emotional, spiritual, or any other aspect of life, his word is always true, and if heeded, leads to godliness.

We are all familiar with the thought that our bodies need the right routine of food, rest, and exercise to run properly and efficiently. If filled up with the wrong fuel of alcohol, drugs, or an excess of the wrong foods, we lose our power; we begin to function improperly and ultimately to "seize up" physically. What we are slower to grasp is that the same is true spiritually. We were also made to run spiritually on the practice of worship, law-keeping, truthfulness, honesty, self-control, discipline, and service to God. If we abandon these things or substitute other things in their place, we progressively *die* spiritually. The conscience dries up, our capacity for truth dwindles, loyalty and honesty are eaten away, and our character begins to disintegrate.

Let's go back to where we began. Is the truth of God's creative word for our benefit? Are God's words of testimony for our benefit? How about his words of command? What about his words of prohibition? Yes, yes, and yes!

If we truly desire to *know* God, then our faith, trust, and obedience must be firmly placed in the truth of his Word and his words! Listen to what God says in his Word about truth:

> "The wrath of God is being revealed from heaven against all the godlessness and wickedness of men who *suppress the truth* by their wickedness, since what may be known about God is plain to them, because God has made it plain to them. For since the creation of the world God's invisible qualities—His eternal power and divine nature—have been clearly seen, being understood from what has been made, so that men are without excuse. For although they knew God, they neither glorified him as God nor gave thanks to Him, but their thinking became futile and their foolish hearts were darkened. Although they claimed to be wise, they became fools and exchanged the glory of the immortal God for images made to look like mortal man and birds and animals and reptiles. Therefore God gave them over in the sinful desires of their hearts to sexual impurity for the degrading of their bodies with one another. *They exchanged the truth of God for a lie,* and worshiped and served created things rather than the Creator—who is

forever praised. Amen. Because of this, God gave them over to shameful lusts. Even their women exchanged natural relations for unnatural ones. In the same way the men also abandoned natural relations with women and were inflamed with lust for one another. Men committed indecent acts with other men, and received in themselves the due penalty for their perversion. Furthermore, since *they did not think it worthwhile to retain the knowledge of God,* He gave them over to a depraved mind, to do what ought not to be done. They have become filled with every kind of wickedness, evil, greed and depravity. They are full of envy, murder, strife, deceit and malice. They are gossips, slanderers, God-haters, insolent, arrogant and boastful; they invent ways of doing evil; they disobey their parents; they are senseless, faithless, heartless, and ruthless. Although they know God's righteous decree that those who do such things deserve death, they not only continue to do these very things but also approve of those who practice them."

Romans 1:18–32

Let me put some of these scriptures together and emphasize the words that have to do with knowing God:

The wrath of God is being revealed from heaven against all the godlessness and wickedness of men who suppress the *truth* by their wickedness. Since what may be *known* about God is plain to them, because God has made it plain to them. Men are without excuse. For although

> they *knew* God, (notice, they knew God ...) they neither glorified him as God nor gave thanks to him. They exchanged the *truth* of God for a lie. Furthermore, since they did not think it worthwhile to *retain the knowledge* of God, He gave them over. Although they *knew* God's righteous decree that those who do such things deserve death, they not only continue to do these things but also approve of those who practice them.

When I think about the knowledge that most people have about God, I find that many people—both inside and outside the church—know many of the stories. And they can name many of the people in God's Word. But somehow they missed the revelation of God himself.

They know about Noah and the Ark, Moses and the Ten Commandments, Daniel in the lion's den, Joseph and his coat of many colors, and of course the Christmas story of Mary, Joseph, and the manger. And they even know that Jesus had twelve disciples, but they don't know God at all! And, of course, they don't know Jesus either. Sometimes I wonder where their information came from. Maybe they remember certain things from their days in Sunday school, or maybe it came from Blockbuster video or from *Jesus Christ Superstar.* But somehow they missed God!

We speak of the last book of the Bible as being the Book of Revelation, but in fact, the Bible, from beginning to end, is a *revelation* of God. His whole purpose in giving us his Word is that we might come to know and understand him better, to really come to "know" him, not just know about him.

Sometimes, I think it would be good to reread the Bible from beginning to end, and after each paragraph or chapter ask the questions: Did you see God? Did you hear God? What was he saying? What was he doing? What was revealed about him? His entire Word is a revelation!

God's Word is not some mysterious book that only preachers can understand. God reveals himself to us in order that we may know and understand him and respond in faith. It begins with believing God is who he says he is! And that he can do what he says he will do! When we understand it, we have to make adjustments in our lives in order to work with him and have a relationship that comes from our experiences with him. Noah could not continue life as usual and build the ark at the same time; he had to make some adjustments. Abraham could not stay in Ur or Haran and father a nation; he had to make some adjustments. God is forever revealing himself or his purpose to those who will listen, believe, and respond by making adjustments in faith.

Our relationship with God must go beyond just knowing a few things about him. It must go beyond just knowing all the good stories in the Bible. It needs to be much deeper than a Sunday morning acquaintance. We need to be at the level of seeing, hearing, feeling, and responding to God whether through his Word, through his Holy Spirit, through people, or circumstances. When we reach that level we can say with confidence that we *know* God.

"Let him who boasts boast of this; that he understands and knows me" says the Lord God Almighty.

LIFE

Mature:

WHERE DO I GROW FROM HERE?

"Until we all reach unity in the faith and in the knowledge of the Son of God and become mature, attaining to the whole measure of the fullness of Christ."

Ephesians 4:13

Part 1:

WHAT ARE YOU BECOMING?

"If anyone else thinks he has reasons to put confidence in the flesh, I have more: circumcised on the eighth day, of the people of Israel, of the tribe of Benjamin, a Hebrew of Hebrews; in regard to the law, a Pharisee; as for zeal, persecuting the church; as for legalistic righteousness, faultless. But whatever was to my profit I now consider loss for the sake of Christ. What is more, I consider everything a loss compared to *the surpassing greatness of knowing Christ Jesus my Lord,* for whose sake I have lost all things. I consider them rubbish, that I may gain Christ and be found in Him, not having a righteousness of my own that comes from the law, but that which is through faith in Christ—the righteousness that comes from God and is by faith. *I want to know Christ and the power of his resurrection* and the fellowship of sharing in his sufferings, becoming like Him in his death, and so, somehow, to attain to the resurrection from the dead. Not that I have already obtained all this, or have already been made perfect, but I press on to take hold of that for which Christ Jesus took hold of me. Brothers, I do not consider myself yet to have taken hold of it. But one thing I do: Forgetting what is behind and straining toward what is ahead, *I press on toward the goal to win the prize for which God has called me heavenward in Christ Jesus. All of us who are mature should take such a view of things.* And if on some point you think differently, that too God will make clear to you. Only let us live up to what we have already attained. Join with others in following my example, brothers, and take note of those who live according to the pattern we gave you. For, as I have often told you before and now say again even with tears, many live as enemies of the cross of Christ. Their destiny is destruction, their god is their stomach, and their glory is in their shame. Their mind is on earthly things. But our citizenship is in heaven. And we eagerly await a Savior from there, the Lord Jesus Christ, who, by the power that enables Him to bring everything under his control, will transform our lowly bodies so that they will be like His glorious body."

Philippians 3:4b–21

"*And this is my prayer: that your love may abound more and more in knowledge and depth of insight,* so that you may be able to discern what is best and may be pure and blameless until the day of Christ, filled with the fruit of righteousness that comes through Jesus Christ—to the glory and praise of God."

Philippians 1:9–11

Those things I have highlighted in these scriptures have to do with knowing and growing in our relationship with Christ. We cannot be followers and "stand still" in our spiritual growth. Like the title of this book says, we are *In it for Life.* This is a lifelong journey.

It is hard to look at any of the Epistle letters and not see the thread of spiritual growth interwoven in the lines somewhere. To young, new Christians, Peter writes, "Like newborn babes, crave spiritual milk, so that by it you may *grow up* in your salvation" (1 Peter 2:2).

In 1 Corinthians 3:1, the Apostle Paul says; "I could not address you as spiritual, but as worldly, mere infants in Christ. I gave you milk, not solid food, for you were not ready for it. Indeed, you still are not ready, you are still worldly." Don't you know that there are still *worldly* Christians in our churches today? There are many who profess to be Christians who have been Christians for many years and still have not grown at all. Because they make no effort to even understand spiritual milk, they will never take in any meat. There are also those who think they don't need any meat; they think they are doing quite well on milk!

Ephesians 4:11 is another example of growth where it says, "The body of Christ is to be built up until we all reach unity in the faith and in the knowledge of the Son of God and become *mature,* attaining to the whole measure of the fullness of God." I look at that statement alone and think that I only have a tablespoon of the full measure of God!

Becoming a mature Christian has nothing to do with how much knowledge you have. Even memorizing the whole Bible won't make you mature. Spiritual maturity is the maturity of a Christlike character. Am

I talking about perfection? No, I'm talking about a process, a lifelong process of discipleship and character growth. Hebrews 10:14 calls it "being sanctified," a work of the Holy Spirit within us. Are you *In it for Life?*

I received some material not long ago on discipleship, and I would like to quote just a couple of parts of that. The first is from Steve DeNeff, one of our Wesleyan Pastors from Michigan.

> "Nearly everything about the local church these days reflects a desire to reach non-Christians. Even the morning worship service; once an hour reserved for adoring and praising and worshipping God; has become our most glamorous opportunity to for introducing Christ. Thus, in many congregations the worship service rivals a great production, complete with all the bells and whistles. However good this may be, and however many people it is reaching, its failure is found in the many "seekers" who come seeking the production and not the product. "Want proof"? He says, "In the past twenty years church growth oriented churches have doled out over fifty billion dollars on church growth materials, conferences and seminars, yet 80% of their growth is by transfer. People are looking for bigger, better, more to offer, churches where they get a bigger bang for their buck! One friend of mine goes to a 9000 member church in Phoenix Arizona that has it's own recreational complex and health spa—for members only—and, has special events going on just about every day of the week. God has called the church to evange-

> lize, for sure, but that's only the first step, not the last. The purpose of the church is not just to produce fruit, but to "produce fruit that will last.""[18]

Charles Colson, author and founder of Prison Fellowship Ministries, says—and rightly so—that:

> "The Great Commission of making disciples involves more than evangelism alone. Though the church must be passionate about leading people to Christ, again, it's only the beginning. There is a life-long process of nurturing and maturing of character that takes place in the church through discipleship.
>
> This discipleship or "growth" comes from several teaching points; it may be the Sunday morning message; it may be the Sunday school time; it may be the mid-week Bible Study or Home groups; It may even be the result of a pre-planned discipleship process of the individual church itself."[19]

This is what *In it for Life* is all about! The point of all this is simply that the church, for the last twenty years has focused almost solely on evangelism without the balance of growth. The result is that we have thousands of people in our churches who say they are saved, but they have never undergone the character transformation that only study and application can bring. Today, we say they are *worldly* Christians. They live, work, think, and act just like they always have. The only thing that has changed is that they enjoy going to church on Sunday.

If you ask them if they consider themselves mature in Christ, their answer would be something along the line of, "Well, I've been a member of this church for thirty years…" But, what if you were to ask them, "Does that mean then that you have attained the whole measure of the fullness of Christ, or that you have just simply grown older along with the church?" I am not pointing any fingers, nor am I trying to make anyone feel guilty; that's the Holy Spirit's job. I am simply saying that spiritual growth is not complete, nor does it end at any certain age of physical maturity or years of church attendance. It ends with perfection. It is only complete when we are perfect, which is when we are Christlike in all things at all times, "filled to the full measure of the fullness of God."

In Philippians 1:6 we read "He who began a good work in you will carry it on to completion." Now we like to quote that as "he who began a good work in you will be faithful to complete it." But it says "he will carry it on to completion until the day of Christ Jesus!" We must be in it for life!

You see, I think there are far too many Christians who are getting older and think they are dying, when God's Word says they ought to be growing and still maturing in Christ. God's not done yet! In fact he says that we are "being renewed day by day," and I don't find any reference to age in that scripture!

If we have lost our energy for spiritual growth it can only be for one of three reasons: (1) we have lost sight of the goal, (2) we think the goal has become unattainable, or (3) we think we have already reached the goal.

Let me elaborate just a little further on this idea of maturity. *Perfect* and *mature* are two English words that have been translated from the same basic Greek word, *teleios.* The word *mature* means "fully developed," while the word *perfect* means "having no flaws or short-comings; to be complete." Though they are very closely related, *mature* and *perfect* are worlds apart. Yet, let me offer this thought: something becomes perfect when it reaches or fulfills its purpose. For example, if your car fulfills all of your expectations of what a car should be, then for you it is a perfect car. In the same way, if your house fulfills all your needs and is everything you expect in a house, then for you it is the perfect house.

Because God created us, Christians then can be said to be *perfect* when we become or fulfill God's expectations of what he created us to be. Our goal then is not just to arrive at heaven's door one day but to become the person and fulfill the purpose that God had in mind when he made us. We are never growing when we are comparing ourselves to one another. We only grow when we compare ourselves to Christ! And when I do that, I find I have a long way to grow!

What Paul says of himself in Philippians 3:13, we must all say if we truly hope to grow in Christ. "Forgetting what is behind"—in the past—whether things we can boast about or things we are ashamed of, it matters not. What matters is that we "press on toward the goal for which God has called us." What matters is not what you were or where you came from. In fact, it really matters not where you are or who you are. *What matters is what you are becoming!*

I challenge you today to look at your life, at your attitudes and your character, and ask yourself; "Where can I grow from here?" "How can I grow from here?"

By the end of this chapter, everyone will have the chance to get "growing" ... no matter what your age!

> "How great is the love the Father has lavished on us, that we should be called children of God! And that is what we are! The reason the world does not know us is that it did not know Him. Dear friends, now we are children of God, and what we will be has not yet been made known. But we know that when He appears, we shall be like Him, for we shall see Him as He is."
>
> 1 John 3:1–3

> "Therefore, since we are surrounded by such a great cloud of witnesses, let us throw off everything that hinders and the sin that so easily entangles, and let us run with perseverance the race marked out for us. Let us fix our eyes on Jesus, the author and perfecter of our faith, who for the joy set before Him endured the cross, scorning its shame, and sat down at the right hand of the throne of God. Consider Him who endured such opposition from sinful men, so that you will not grow weary and lose heart." ... "Endure hardship as discipline; God is treating you as sons. For what son is not disciplined by his father? If you are not disciplined, and everyone undergoes discipline, then you are illegitimate children and not true sons. Moreover, we have all had human fathers who disciplined us and we respected them for it. How much more should we submit to the Father of our spirits and live! Our fathers disciplined us

> for a little while as they thought best; but God disciplines us for our good, that we may share in his holiness. No discipline seems pleasant at the time, but painful. Later on, however, it produces a harvest of righteousness and peace for those who have been trained by it."
>
> Hebrews 12:1–11

I want to begin this section by telling a short, hypothetical story. This story is about a six-year-old boy we'll call "Kevin." Kevin decides he wants to play the guitar. His parents sign him up for lessons, and after school each day, he sits and strums his guitar, slowly learning the chords. After a while of doing this every day and watching all his buddies play baseball in the park across the street, Kevin gets bored, and the discipline of practice becomes drudgery.

Now suppose Kevin is visited by an angel one afternoon during his practice and is taken in a vision to Carnegie Hall. He sees a guitar virtuoso giving a concert. While usually bored by classical music, Kevin is absolutely astonished by what he sees and hears. The musician's fingers dance fluidly over the strings with ease and grace. Kevin thinks about how stupid and clunky his hands feel while trying to play even a single chord. But Kevin is enchanted and never imagined anyone could play guitar like this! "What do you think?" the angel asks Kevin. All Kevin can say is, "*Wow.*" The vision vanishes, and Kevin is once again sitting on the couch in his living room.

"Kevin," says the angel, "the wonderful music you just heard and saw is you in a few years." Then pointing to the guitar, the angel says "But you must discipline yourself to practice, practice, practice!"

Do you think Kevin's attitude about practice will be different now? I think it will, as long as he remembers the vision of what he is going to become! "What we will be has not yet been made known" (1 John 3:2). When it comes to discipline in the Christian life and lifestyle, many of us feel like Kevin did toward his guitar practice. At first it is fun and even interesting, and we are learning new stuff and trying new things. But it isn't long before we become bored and especially tired of the repetition, and we figure "as long as we know the basics" that's all that matters.

However, perhaps, like Kevin, we need to understand or gain the vision of what we shall become! Our scripture says we "shall be like him." And verse three says that "everyone who has this hope in him purifies himself, just as he is pure." If I may put that in my own words, I would say, "If we have seen and have hope in the vision of what we shall become, it ought to motivate us to practice!"

Romans 8:29 tells us that "those God foreknew he also predestined to be conformed" (not transformed but conformed, there is a difference) "to the image or likeness of his Son." This is God's eternal plan; for us to grow into that likeness. Part of that process is allowing God to *conform* us or shape us as we practice, practice, practice!

Let me remind you of something very important about God's Word. In the book of Genesis, it says that God spoke, and many things were *created.* Now don't miss this. It goes on to say that God *formed* man out of the dust of the earth. Man was *formed* by the hands of God into his likeness. Man fell into sin, and that likeness was *deformed.* The rest of the Bible is about God showing us how we can be *conformed* back into his likeness!

In 1 Timothy 4:7, it is explained very clearly: "Discipline yourselves for the purpose of godliness. For physical training is of some value, but godliness"—or Christlikeness—"has value for both this life and the life to come."

I am talking about the disciplines in life that promote spiritual growth. They are what I would call the "habits" of devotion that have been practiced by people of God for over 2000 years. We can think of it this way: there is little value in practicing chords on the guitar apart from the purpose of playing music. There is also *little value in practicing Christianity apart from the purpose of Christlikeness.*

Actually, God uses three primary catalysts for conforming us, other than his Word, but only one of the three is under our control. The first is *other people.* Proverb 27:17 says, "As iron sharpens iron, so one man sharpens another." God may use our friends, our family, our coworkers, our pastor, our Sunday school teacher, and he may even use people we don't like to file away our rough edges.

The second way God conforms us is through *circumstances.* Romans 8:28 says, "We know in all things God works for the good of those who love him, who have been called according to his purpose." Whether financial pressures, physical conditions, or even the weather itself, in divine hands, all things can be used to conform us. Think of the story of the Disciples in the storm. God was conforming them through a simple lesson in faith.

When God changes or conforms us through people or circumstances, the process works from the outside in. However, the third catalyst is found within ourselves. You see, we have little control over the way people or circumstances affect our lives, but we make the decision whether or not we will attend church or Bible study. We decide whether or not we will read or study God's Word during the week or spend each morning in devotions and prayer. It's our will that changes or conforms us from the inside out. As it concerns our will, it always makes me think of the street in an area where we used to live back in Wisconsin called Lackawanna!

All three of these are channels by which God's grace, power, knowledge, and wisdom flow to us and through us to conform our will. Think about this: most often it is the conforming of our will that is the least painful and the most rewarding in life, if we would only change our "Lackawanna."

Sometimes being a pastor is a lot like the way Tom Landry—once coach of the Dallas Cowboys—described his job. "The job of a coach is to make men do what they don't want to do in order to help them to become what they really want to be!" And that requires discipline.

Whether it's playing the guitar, playing football, becoming an expert carpenter, a successful business man, or a master mom, we can decide that it's just too much work and not worth the effort or we can forget what we are, think about what we shall become, and discipline ourselves to do what it takes to get there!

You see, discipline without direction is drudgery. Remember Kevin? His daily practice takes on a whole new spirit once he realized what he could become! If your vision of a disciplined Christian life is a grim, tight-lipped, joyless, half-robot, mixture of lemon and prunes kind of person, you've missed the point! That kind of person is more like pepper rather than salt in the world!

2 Peter 1:3–12 says,

> "His divine power has given us everything we need for life and godliness through our knowledge of Him who called us by His own glory and goodness. Through these He has given us very great and precious promises, so that through them you may participate in the divine nature and escape the corruption in the world caused by evil desires."

Now, notice the progression of growth here:

> "For this very reason, make every effort to *add* to your faith goodness; and to goodness knowledge; and to knowledge self-control; and to self-control perseverance; and to perseverance godliness; and to godliness brotherly kindness; and to brotherly kindness love. For if you possess these things in *increasing measure;* they will keep you from being ineffective and unproductive in your knowledge of our Lord Jesus Christ."

Notice also that we can lose sight of what we shall become:

> "But, if anyone does not have them, he is near-sighted and blind, and has forgotten that he has been cleansed from his past sins. Therefore, my brothers, be all the more eager to make your calling and election sure. For if you do these things you will never fall, and you will receive a rich welcome into the eternal kingdom of our Lord and Savior, Jesus Christ. So, I will always remind you of these things, even though you know them and are firmly established in the truth you now have."

Sometimes we need spiritual reminders. We need to take a look at our spiritual walk and ask ourselves, "Where can I grow from here?" Discipline!

Part 2:

FIVE DISCIPLINES OF GROWTH

"And we know that in all things God works for the good of those who love Him, who have been called according to His purpose. For those God foreknew He also predestined to be conformed to the likeness of His Son."

Romans 8:28–29

"Therefore, my dear friends, as you have always obeyed—not only in my presence, but now much more in my absence—continue to work out your salvation with fear and trembling, for it is God who works in you to will and to act according to His good purpose."

Philippians 2:12–13

In this chapter, we are looking at growth. More specifically, the kind of growth that is given in Ephesians 4:16 where it says that we are to "become mature, attaining to the whole measure of the fullness of

Christ." This scripture from Romans 8:29 tells us that "Those God has called, he has predestined: to be *conformed* to the likeness of Christ his Son." That is, to develop a Christlike character as we strive to fulfill God's expectations and his purpose for our lives.

The Apostle Paul said that he had "not yet attained this goal," and we are encouraged to "press on," "straining" for the goal, until the day of Christ. In other words, we are never to stop growing, never stop trying, and never quit in the middle of the race, nor are we to think we have attained this goal, "until the day of Christ."

While it may be true that some are more mature and Christlike in character than others, that's not the goal! The measure of our growth is not one another! It is Christ and Christ alone! He is the standard; he is the plumb bob, his likeness is the goal, and compared to Christ, we have a long way to grow.

The encouraging thing about our spiritual growth is that we don't have to think we are alone in this seemingly impossible walk. The fact is that we can't do it on our own, nor should we expect God to do it for us. You could say it is a partnership. We must do our part, and God will do his. In this scripture from Philippians 2:12, it says "continue to work out your salvation with fear and trembling;" that's our part! "For it is God who works in you to will and to act according to his good purpose;" that's God's part. God continues to work *in us,* as we do our part and continue to practice, practice, practice!

Let me say that to "work out our salvation" has nothing to with salvation by works. "It is by grace you have been saved, through faith, not by works, lest any man should boast" (Ephesians 2:8–9). Good works are an expression of, or a manifestation of, our salvation. We are good and do good, because we are saved, not in order to be saved. This then, is an expression to *carry on* or *continue to grow in* or *work out* our salvation.

At the same time, and probably at the same rate that we are growing, God works in us changing our attitudes, actions, and desires. He is changing our "have-to's" into "want to's"! You see, there is a difference between someone who feels they "have to" do something and a person who "wants to" do something. Whether it is an athlete, a musician, or a growing Christian, they don't have to practice and discipline their lives, if they don't want to! But, if their goal is to be very good, or even the best at what they are doing, they will want to! That's what God is doing *in* us. He is trying to change our will, our "Lackawanna." "It is God who works in you to will and to act." He wants to partner with us and to help us to see the goal of becoming the best we can be.

You can tell someone is an athlete when they train, practice, and discipline themselves to do more than run around the dinner table. You can tell someone is a musician when they practice and discipline themselves to play more than chopsticks. You can tell someone is a Christian when ...? You can finish the sentence.

Let's say that you and God are going to make a trip down the "river of life," and your goal is "Paradise Island." Now the first thing you must do is get in the canoe. We call that salvation. So you and God are both in the canoe, heading toward Paradise Island. But you decide that you don't want to paddle. You are going to let God do all the paddling, and if you are going to get to Paradise Island, God will have to do all the work! You just expect that he is going to keep the canoe headed in the right direction, and you are just going to go along for the ride! Does that sound crazy? But that's how some Christians are going through life. They don't *want* to discipline themselves in any way! "If it's going to be, then God will have to do it" is their attitude.

Now suppose God works on you a little bit, and you decide you probably should do something at least. But you don't listen to God's directions, you just stick your paddle in the water and make like you're doing something. But the canoe just seems to go in circles! You can see Paradise Island every once in a while, when the canoe spins in that direction, but for the most part, you don't really know what direction you are supposed to be going. That's the way some other Christians are!

Wouldn't it be much easier if we allowed God to "work in us to *will* and to *act*," according to his purpose and direction? Of course it would. We must do our part, keeping our eyes on the goal, and practicing what he tells us, and God will do his part. By the way, I can tell you from experience, our part becomes less burdensome when we realize we have the infinite energy and power of God working with us!

An incident in one of the rivers of New York would be a good example. The building of a bridge was interrupted, because of a sunken ship in the bottom of the river was in the way. Divers went down and hooked chains and cables to the ship, and powerful tugs tried to dislodge it; but it wouldn't budge. Then a young technical-school student asked if he could give some advice. His solution was simple. He took flatboat barges, which the workers were working on, and when the tide was out, fastened them to the sunken ship. Then, when the tide came in, it lifted the flatboats and, of course, lifted the sunken ship. He accomplished a seemingly impossible task by harnessing the infinite power of the ocean.[20]

Everything about the Christian walk is a partnership. Even I am a partner with you in this growth process. Listen again to Ephesians 4:11, "It was he who gave some to be pastors and teachers, to prepare God's people for works of service, so that the body of Christ may be built up until we all become mature, attaining to the whole measure of the fullness of Christ." So, not only is God a partner working in you, but as a pastor and teacher, I am a partner working *with* you! But there is more. Ephesians 4:15–16 says, "Speaking the truth in love, we will in all things grow up into Him who is the head, that is Christ. From Him, the whole body grows and builds itself up in love, as *each part does its work.*" You see, you are a partner as well. We are all partners with one another. We are to help one another grow. As each part grows, the whole body grows. And, as the body grows, each part grows. It's an ongoing process.

It is God's will that we be conformed into Christ's likeness; that's the goal. He wants to help us in this process, and he wants us to help one another in this process. The Bible says that we are a temple in which the Spirit of God dwells. Let's not be satisfied being a cute, little cottage, when God is trying to build a temple. Let's not be satisfied with chopsticks, when God wants us to be concert musicians. Let's not feel like we have to attend church or Bible study or like we have to read God's Word and pray; let's allow God to change all that into a "*wanna!*"

Here is another scripture from Ephesians 3:14, which is the Apostle Paul's prayer for us.

> "For this reason I kneel before the Father, from whom his whole family in heaven and on earth derives its name. I pray that out of his glorious riches He may strengthen you with power through His Spirit in your inner being, so that Christ may dwell in your hearts through faith. And, I pray that you, being rooted and established in love, may have power together with all the saints, to grasp how wide and long and high and deep is the love of Christ, and to know this love that surpasses knowledge, that you may be filled to the measure of all the fullness of God."

And do you know what the last two verses are? My favorite benediction.

> "Now, unto Him who is able to do immeasurably more than all that we ask or imagine, according to His power that is at work within us, to Him be the glory in the church and in Christ Jesus throughout all generations, forever and forever, Amen."

In all that we say, in all that we do, we are to do it as unto the Lord. The Bible says that we are his masterpiece. We are his workmanship. We are created in Christ Jesus to do good works!

There are many things we must discipline ourselves to do along this journey of growth, but none is more important than the intake of God's Word. The intake of God's Word really involves more than we think. It involves the five disciplines of hearing, reading, study, meditation, and prayer. Hearing may come through preaching, teaching, tapes, or music—all of which enter our ears. Reading of course is just that, a daily or consistent reading of God's Word. Study, however, involves more than just reading. There are many ways to study the Bible. I personally like the "tree" approach. This is where step one is just a general reading of scripture. It's kind of like standing and looking at a tree. The second step is choosing a book of the Bible. This will be the "trunk" of the tree. The third step is a chapter by chapter study. This is like a close study of the "limbs" of the tree. The fourth step is a paragraph study like the "branches" on the limb of the tree. And the fifth step would be a *word* study or checking out each "leaf." Most people are satisfied with just looking at the tree! And, for many, it's just a quick glance. However, when you combine all of these steps together, they bring a deeper, fuller, sweeter, understanding God's Word. The point is that all of this must lead us to application. Information without application is just knowledge. There can be no healthy Christian life of growth without the milk and the meat of the scriptures being our constant nutrition.

Well, back to the five disciplines. When it comes to the intake of God's Word, the easiest is *hearing,* because all you have to do is sit and listen! For most of us, that means attending a New Testament church where the Word of God is faithfully preached. Jesus said, "Blessed are those who hear the Word of God and obey it." Paul said in Romans 10:17, "Consequently, faith comes by hearing, and hearing by the Word of God." That means that initial faith in Jesus Christ comes by hearing the inspired word about Christ from God's Word. The faith we need for life comes from hearing this Word! Now there are other ways we can "hear" God's Word. The most obvious would be TV, radio, and tapes. All of these may be good, if we are really listening and if we know we are listening to the truth! But nothing is better than a live presentation!

Paul, once again in 1 Timothy 4:13, instructs Timothy to "devote himself to the public reading of scripture, and to preaching and teaching." Why? To insure that the people would at least hear the Word of God, and that by hearing they might have faith.

In those days, the people were actually encouraged not to read the scriptures. The Pharisees and other religious leaders felt the common person could not understand, and there were no book stores! The Scriptures were not as readily available as we have today. The Pharisees, as Jesus pointed out to them, had a "do-as-I-say-and-not-as-I-do" religion.

The problem is that it is proven that we retain very little of what we hear! And, like those in the Parable of the Sower, Satan quickly snatches away what may have been sown, and we soon forget. Need proof? How many of you heard the preacher's message two weeks ago? Or better yet, how many heard the preacher's message last week? And how much do you remember? You see, *hearing* alone will not promote spiritual growth. It will and *does encourage our faith,* but hearing alone will not promote the kind of growth we need for *life.*

One thing that will help of course is if we actually "read" God's Word. I'm talking about a daily intake of reading God's Word. Ask yourself this question; "Where did I put my Bible when I got home from church last week, and where was it when I picked it up this Sunday morning?" If the answer is the same for both questions, it may be because you never moved it! There was a survey taken by the Barna Research Group among those who claim to be born-again Christians. It was disclosed that only eighteen percent read their Bible on a daily basis. Eighteen percent! Worse yet, twenty-three percent said that they "very seldom" read the Bible on their own. Consider that in the light of the lack of spiritual growth in our churches today.

Did you know that Jesus often asked questions about people's understanding of the Scriptures? He would often begin his teaching with the words: "Have you not read?" or "Have you not heard?" He assumed that those who claimed to be people of God would have at least read the Word of God! According to 2 Timothy 3:16, "All scripture is God breathed and useful for teaching, rebuking, correcting, and training in righteousness," so it just makes sense that we ought to read it, and read it on a daily basis, in order to grow! Let me ask this question: "How often do we face problems in life? How often do we encounter temptations? When are we faced with pressure and decisions in life? The answer is every day! How often then do we need God's Word?

D.L. Moody put it this way: "A man can no more take in a supply of grace for the future in one Sunday than he can eat enough in one meal to sustain him for six months! Or take in enough air in his lungs to sustain him for a week. We must draw on God's source of grace and guidance every day."

Revelation 1:3 says; "Blessed is the one who *reads* the words of prophecy, and blessed are those who *hear* it and *take to heart* what is written in it, because the time is near."

Well, if hearing the Word, and reading the Word promotes healthy growth, then what do you think is the value of study? If reading the Bible is compared to cruising across a lake in a motorboat, then study is like slowly crossing that same lake in a glass-bottom boat. It takes us beneath the surface of scripture and gives us a clarity, detail, and understanding, which are certainly missed by just hearing and reading.

When I was on a mission trip in Jamaica, the Caribbean Ocean was much different than the ocean at Myrtle Beach, North Carolina. Not only was the water clearer and a different color, but I actually went out in a glass-bottom boat and got to observe everything beneath the surface with great clarity. I saw things on the coral reefs I never knew existed!

Our study of God's Word may be going through some kind of study guide on our own, or it may be a fellowship of study as most churches have on Wednesday or Sunday evenings. But the point is that we need a more *in-depth* study and understanding of God's Word in order to truly understand God himself and his conforming purpose of shaping us into Christlikeness. Our growth is greatly affected by the quality and the quantity of our intake of God's Word.

In his magnificent prayer in John 17, Jesus said,

"Sanctify them by the truth; your Word is truth." God's plan for sanctifying us, for setting us apart, or making us holy and godly is accomplished by the means of the truth of his Word. If we settle for a poor quality of just hearing, seldom reading, and not studying at all, we severely restrict the life-giving flow of nourishment, which causes us to grow, and we become "stunted" in our growth.

I said that there were five important disciplines of spiritual growth, and we have covered three. Next, we will look at meditation and prayer. However, I hope you can see the importance of even these three: hearing, reading, and study and how together they will make us healthier Christians then any one of them alone. And, add to that, meditation and prayer, which not only helps in the growth process, but also increases and enhances our relationship with God, and you have exactly what it takes to conform us into Christlikeness, which is God's purpose and desire.

> Listen to the theme of *meditation* ... "Blessed are they whose ways are blameless, who walk according to the law of the Lord. Blessed are they who keep His statutes and seek him with all their heart. I will praise you with an upright heart as I learn your righteous laws. I have hidden your Word in my heart that I might not sin against you. I rejoice in following your statutes as one rejoices in great riches. I *meditate* on your precepts and consider your ways. I delight in your decrees; I will not neglect Your Word. Open my eyes that I might see wonderful things in your law. Though rulers sit together and slander me,

> your servant will *meditate* on your decrees. Your statutes are my delight; they are my counselors. Teach me your decrees, let me understand the teaching of your precepts. Give me understanding, and I will keep your law and obey it with all my heart … for I trust in Your Word."
>
> Psalm 119:1,2,7,11,14,15,16,18,23,24,26,27,34,42b

In Joshua 1:7–8, God says to Joshua,

> "Be strong and very courageous. Be careful to obey all the law my servant Moses gave you; do not turn from it to the right or to the left, that you may be successful wherever you go. Do not let this Book of the Law depart from your mouth; *meditate* on it day and night, so that you may be careful to do everything written in it. Then you will be prosperous and successful."

Once again, 2 Peter 1:5 tells that we are to "make every effort to add to our faith goodness; and to goodness, knowledge." However, as good as faith and knowledge are, if that's all there is, it will still fall short in the *conforming process* of God. When it comes to biblical knowledge, there are many who would blow the socks off this pastor at Bible trivia. The problem is that they haven't grown much at all spiritually.

Now to hearing, which brings faith, and reading, which brings knowledge, you were to add study and meditation, and you would be on the path to *wisdom* and true growth!

It is in the study of God's Word—whether personal or corporate—that we gain "insight and understanding," which brings *wisdom.* We only have to turn to the book of Proverbs to know how important wisdom is to our lives; I challenge you to take the time and just read the first four chapters of Proverbs. Go ahead; put this book down, and do it!

Anytime you see the word *meditate* in God's Word, you will usually find the word *pray* or *prayer.* That's because the two go hand in hand. *To meditate* means to "intentionally ponder or reflect upon or focus on something." While there are some groups out there, which advocate the kind of meditation in which you do your best to "empty" your mind, biblical meditation has to do with *filling* your mind! Psalm 1:1–3 says, "Blessed is the man who does not walk in the counsel of the wicked or stand in the way of sinners, or sit in the seat of mockers, but, his delight is in the law of the Lord, and on his law he *meditates*"—at least once a year? No. At least once a month? No. "D*ay and night,*" it says! "He is like a tree planted by streams of water, which yields its fruit in season and whose leaf does not wither." Why? Because it has a constant source of living water!

Let me add this from Philippians 4:8, which gives us an idea of the kinds of things we ought to meditate on: "Whatever is true, whatever is noble, whatever is right, whatever is pure, whatever is lovely or admirable, if anything is excellent or praiseworthy, think about, (or meditate on) such things." Wouldn't it be wonderful to meditate on these things rather than our problems all the time?

Here are four reasons we need to *intentionally* set aside time for meditation:

- In order to understand God's Word.
- In order to understand God.
- In order to understand life and the events of life.
- In order to understand God's will.

What are the first four common words here? "In order to understand." With understanding comes wisdom!

The other part of this discipline involves prayer. Prayer is more than just asking for something; it is also more than just talking to God. Prayer opens us up to the Holy Spirit's illumination and intensifies our spiritual perception. It's like a TV antenna, which puts us on God's spiritual wavelength and prepares us to receive... and not just transmit!

The Bible was written under the Holy Spirit's inspiration, and many cannot understand it without the Holy Spirit's illumination. 1 Corinthians 2:14 tells us, "The man without the Spirit does not accept the things that come from the Spirit of God, for they are foolishness to him, and he cannot understand them, because they are spiritually discerned." We need to also know that prayer ought to always precede meditation, as well as hearing, reading, and study, because it plugs us in to the source of understanding.

Well, where do I grow from here? Perhaps a better question might be "How do I grow from here?" If you are diligently seeking all five disciplines of hearing, reading, study, meditation, and prayer, as much as it concerns God's Word, you are well on your way to being "conformed into the likeness of Christ." But, if you are missing out on any of these five disciplines, you are "stunting" your growth. You are hindering the process by which God desires to work in your life. Therefore you become like a spiritual bonsai tree. And even more than that, you are missing out on the greatest blessing in the world, worth more than all the gold in Fort Knox. That is the blessing of knowing and experiencing God in your life everyday!

Be-Loved:

GOD MEASURES CHRISTIANS, AS WELL AS CHURCHES, BY HOW MUCH WE ARE LEARNING TO LOVE ONE ANOTHER.

"A new command I give you: Love one another. As I have loved you, so you must love one another. By this all men will know that you are my disciples, if you love one another."

John 13:34–35

Introduction:

WHAT THE BIBLE SAYS ABOUT "LOVE"

"Dear friends, *let us love one another,* for love comes from God. Everyone who loves has been born of God and knows God. Whoever does not love does not know God, because God is love. This is how God showed his love among us: He sent his one and only Son into the world that we might live through Him. This is love: not that we loved God, but that He loved us and sent His Son as an atoning sacrifice for our sins. Dear friends, since God so loved us, we also ought to *love one another.* No one has ever seen God; but *if we love one another,* God lives in us and His love is made complete in us."

1 John 4:7

"A new command I give you: *Love one another.* As I have loved you, so you must *love one another.* By this all men will know that you are My disciples, *if you love one another.*"

John 13:34

"This is the message you heard from the beginning: We should *love one another*... Do not be surprised, my brothers, if the world hates you. We know that we have passed from death to life, because we *love our brothers.*... Dear children, let us not love with words or tongue but with actions and in truth... And this is His command: to believe in the name of His Son, Jesus Christ, and to *love one another* as He commanded us."

1 John 3:11–23

"God is love. Whoever lives in love lives in God, and God in him. In this way, love is made complete among us so that we will have confidence on the day of judgment, because in this world we are like Him. There is no fear in love. But *perfect love drives out fear,* because fear has to do with punishment. The one who fears is not made perfect in love. *We love because he first loved us.* If anyone says, "I love God," yet hates his brother, he is a liar. For anyone who does not love his brother, whom he has seen, cannot love God, whom he has not seen. And He has given us this command: *Whoever loves God must also love his brother.*"

1 John 4:16–21

> "If I speak in the tongues of men and of angels, but have not love, I am only a resounding gong or a clanging cymbal. If I have the gift of prophecy and can fathom all mysteries and all knowledge, and if I have a faith that can move mountains but have not love, I am nothing. If I give all I possess to the poor and surrender my body to the flames, but have not love, I gain nothing. Love is patient, love is kind. It does not envy, it does not boast, it is not proud. It is not rude, it is not self-seeking, it is not easily angered, it keeps no record of wrongs. Love does not delight in evil but rejoices with the truth. It always protects, always trusts, always hopes, always perseveres. Love never fails ... And now these three remain: faith, hope and love. But the *greatest of these is love.*"
>
> 1 Corinthians 13:1–7 and 13

> "Teacher, which is the greatest commandment in the Law?" Jesus replied: "Love the Lord your God with all your heart and with all your soul and with all your mind. This is the first and greatest commandment. And the second is like it: *Love your neighbor as yourself.*"
>
> Matthew 22:36–37

With all this in mind, let me take you to Ephesians 4:1–16:

> "As a prisoner for the Lord, then, I urge you to live a life worthy of the calling you have received. Be completely humble and gentle; be

> patient, bearing with one another in love ... until we all reach unity in the faith and in the knowledge of the Son of God and become mature, attaining to the whole measure of the fullness of Christ ... Instead, speaking the truth in love, we will in all things grow up into Him who is the head, that is, Christ. From Him the whole body, joined and held together by every supporting ligament, *grows and builds itself up in love,* as each part does its work."

Did you catch that? Let me repeat it again: "the whole body, joined and held together by every supporting ligament, *grows and builds itself up in love!*"

> The church, the Body of Christ, that is functioning properly, will be a place where all people can come to learn to give and receive *love.* Something they won't find in the world, and many not even find in their own families.

When Paul wrote to the Corinthian church, he said, "And now abide faith, hope, and love, these three; but the greatest of these is love." Without question, love is the greatest mark of maturity in a Christian, as well as in the church. There is so much written about love in the Bible that volumes have been preached on the subject, and volumes more could be written. Jesus said, "A new command I give you: *Love one another.* As I have loved you, so you must *love one another.* By this all men will know that you are my disciples, *if you love one another*" (John 13:34–35).

Do you think he was trying to make a point?

Paul goes on to tells us that we can do all kinds of wonderful things in and with our lives, but if we have not love, we are nothing. This mark of maturity is related to the very essence of God himself. "God is love. Whoever lives in love lives in God, and God in him. Love is made complete among us so that we will have confidence on the Day of Judgment, because in this world we are like Him" (1 John 4:16–17).

In this same scripture Paul lists ten qualities of love that we are to have in our lives: (1) "Love is patient:" We have ample opportunities to develop and demonstrate patience in our lives every time we are frustrated or angry, (2) "Love is kind:" Kindness is an act of the will, which is generated by positive feelings. We are seldom kind to someone we have negative feelings for. (3) "Love does not envy:" Spiritual maturity means that we do not compare ourselves to one another, what we have or don't have. We compare ourselves to Christ and Christ alone. (4) "Love does not boast:" Humility involves considering the needs and interests of others above our own, and never thinking we are better than anyone else. (5) "Love is not rude:" It involves being courteous or "turning the other cheek," when we are irritated or we disagree. (6) "Love is not self-seeking:" We live in a selfish world that is constantly thinking only of self-pleasure and a me-first mentality. (7) "Love is not easily angered:" This quality of maintaining our emotional balance, staying calm and cool, may require intense discipline. (8) "Love keeps no record of wrongs:" A record of wrongs is an unforgiven past, and is like a festering sore that destroys happiness and well-being in the present and the future. (9) "Love does not delight in evil, but rejoices with the truth:"

Love keeps its motives pure. It holds righteousness, honesty, integrity, and truth above all else, and, finally, I will say (10) "Love is a commitment:" Look at the word *always,* "it always protects, always trusts, always hopes, always perseveres ... Love never fails!"

Love is the means that God designed to separate Christians from the world. It is also a scriptural way to recognize discipleship. Of everything I have mentioned so far, love is the most measurable part of our Christian growth. How do we measure love in our lives? Simply insert your name in front of the ten qualities of love I just listed and see if you measure up!

If you read 1 Corinthians 13 again, it won't take long to realize that the world has become everything that Paul says love is not. It certainly has not become what love is! But then, we must ask ourselves has the church become what love is?

Jesus gave a command to the body to "love one another." This chapter will show how we can do just that and so fulfill the command of Christ in the church. To begin, we must realize that this is a command of Jesus. It's not an opinion; it's not a suggestion; it's not an option! And, because it is a command, we should also realize that neither God nor Jesus would ask us to do something that we would not be enabled or empowered to accomplish.

Jesus also said, "This is how they will know you are my disciples, by your love for one another." I think love, and the degree to which we are growing in our love for one another, is how God measures us individually, as well as the church. In his letter to the Thessalonians church Paul writes, "We always thank God for all of you, mentioning you in our prayers. We continually remember before our God and Father your work produced by faith, your labor prompted by *love,* and your endurance inspired by hope in our Lord Jesus Christ." And, in his second letter, he says "We ought always to thank God for you, brothers, and rightly so, because your faith is growing more and more, and *the love every one of you has for each other is increasing.*" A growing faith and an ever-increasing love are important factors to Paul, and I'm sure they are to God as well.

Well, I can just see the disciples looking at each other thinking: "Love one another?" "It's easy for him to say!" "How are we supposed to love one another?" The answer is found in all of the "one another's" in the New Testament. They are our guidelines to follow; and our steps to growth in true Christian love.

I have chosen twelve out of the nineteen or twenty-some "one another's" in the New Testament, because several are so closely related. These are the way of love. These show us how to translate the command to "love one another" into concrete and specific actions. I have found that these "one another" actions can be divided into three specific groups. The first I will call Foundational Guidelines. This is because they are foundational in all of our relationships and especially in the church. We will look at each one as we go through this chapter, but for now I will just list them:

Foundational Guidelines:

1. (Romans 15:7): "Accept *one another*"
2. (Romans 12:10): "Be devoted to *one another*"

3. (Romans 12:16): "Live in harmony with *one another*"
4. (Ephesians 4:2 and Colossians 3:13): "Bear with *one another*"

I think you can already see how these four would affect our relationships, as well as the church.

The second group are Sustaining Guidelines; these are what "sustains" all our relationships, and especially within the church:

1. (Colossians. 3:13 and Ephesians 4:32): "Forgive *one another*"
2. (James 5:16): "Confess and Pray for *one another*"
3. (Galatians 5:13): "Serve *one another*"
4. (I Thessalonians 5:11): "Encourage *one another*" and "Build *one another* up"

Can you see this coming together? The third group is the Crisis Guidelines, because they involve times of "crisis" in our relationships:

1. (Galatians 6:2): "Bear *one another's* burdens"
2. (I Thessalonians 4:18): "Comfort *one another*"
3. (Hebrews 10:24): "Spur *one another* on"
4. (Colossians 3:16): "Teach and admonish *one another*"

All of these are given to show us how to truly fulfill the command to "love one another." This is what it takes to build, grow, and sustain relationships. Remember, "this is how they"—which is the world—"will know that you are my disciples," says Jesus. I believe this is something worthy of our attention!

Part 1:

UNITY IN DIVERSITY

Before we can get into these guidelines, I think we must first decide if we can learn to *Love Across Our Differences?* [21] This is the title of a book by Gerald Sittser, which I have used as a reference to this very subject.

The church, as we know it today, is characterized by denominations: a variety of ethnic backgrounds, different social standing, diversity of ideas, distrust, disagreement, and yes, division. Yet, there is a call for unity. What does love require in a pluralistic church where we are required to "Love the Lord our God, and our neighbor as ourselves?" How should we handle differences in the church: different opinions, different ideas, and even different beliefs? On one side are the conservatives, on the other are the liberals, and everything in between! I mean, how should Christians handle theological, ethical, moral, and even economical controversy and diversity in the church?

A practicing homosexual wants to join a conservative church and is turned away. A popular church elder divorces his wife and starts to date someone from the same church. A division develops in the church as some people are pro-choice and others are pro-life. How in the world can Christians learn to love one another and develop unity in spite of our differences?

Well, Professor Sittser offers three options that appear to be possible. The first, he says, is to "try and accept diversity and embrace tolerance." But this is troublesome from a Biblical point of view, because that would mean there are no standards of belief, conduct, or character, to which all Christians should measure up. I must agree with him when he says, "Political correctness cannot become the standard for the church!"

The second option is that we could "eliminate diversity and strive for 'oneness.'" However, that would demand judgment, discipline, and conformity. Who is going to decide what that "oneness" should be? It seems to me that this would even further divide the church.

The third option is that we could strive for unity in our diversity. This would be very demanding and difficult because it requires sacrifice, servanthood, and compromise; but it is the way of love! It is the way that Jesus commands, and he gives us some guidelines that will help us do just that.

Before we can focus on these "one another" scriptures, we need to settle our thinking about diversity, of which there are two kinds: One is the diversity of belief as it concerns "issues." This surfaces in differences of theological, ethical, moral, and political opinion. In our world, in which we live today, Christians are either *soldiers,* or they are *casualties* in the fight over abortion, homosexuality, inerrancy of scripture, speaking in tongues, baptism, civil or social rights, and the list goes on!

The second kind of diversity is not about issues as much as it is about *style.* These are the little things that frustrate and irritate us in and about the church. Things like style of music, style of worship and how to spend money, what to do about the kids in the church, who should or should not be in areas of leadership, and for that matter, who should or should not be welcomed as a member!

Listen, quantity and quality of love are not the issue. The real issue is our *selectivity.* We think we have the right and duty to decide who to love and how to love them! But the Bible does not give us that right. It *commands* us to love one another and attaches no conditions whatsoever to the command. The Apostle Paul reasoned that the cross of Christ breaks down all dividing walls. It clears out a piece of level ground at the foot of the cross where we all stand equal, sinners and saints in need of the grace of God.

This leads us to the first Foundational Guideline: "Accept one another."

Part 2:

FOUNDATIONAL GUIDELINES

God wants us to "accept one another" (Romans 15:7). He wants us to give each other the slack and the room to grow that he has given us. He wants us to give each other room to mature in our spiritual walk and in our relationship with him at our own pace, room to be who we are and allow God to shape others into what he wants them to be! We need to give each other room to contribute who we are and what we are to the church and to the world, in spite of our imperfections. It gives us the room to recognize that we are all clay in the hands of the "potter" and we are all a work in progress!

Accepting one another must be done without communicating a spirit of disapproval or judgment. To *accept one another* means that we do not claim the right to remake others into copies of ourselves. We do not dictate how they live or believe.

> "Accept him whose faith is weak, without passing judgment on disputable matters. One man's

> faith allows him to eat everything, but another man, whose faith is weak, eats only vegetables. The man who eats everything must not look down on him who does not, and the man who does not eat everything must not condemn the man who does, for God has accepted him. Who are you to judge someone else's servant? To his own master he stands or falls. And he will stand, for the Lord is able to make him stand."
>
> Romans 14:1–4

> "So then, each of us will give an account of himself to God. Therefore let us stop passing judgment on one another. Instead, make up your mind not to put any stumbling block or obstacle in your brother's way."
>
> Romans 14:12–13

Romans 14:19–20 says this: "Let us therefore make every effort to do what leads to peace and to mutual edification. Do not destroy the work of God for the sake of __________."

Paul is talking about food that is sacrificed to idols, but we could fill in that blank with just about anything. How about *the color of the carpet, the style of music, dress, or hairstyle,* or any other trivial thing we can think of that can—and does—destroy the work of God! Not only can these things destroy the work of God in a church but in an individual as well.

In my early childhood, I had a teacher who seemed to have the ability to discern and value the personality of each individual child. She communicated a spirit of acceptance and genuine care about the future of each one. She never showed preference of "bright" over "slow," "coy" over "assertive," or "serious" over "silly;" and consequently, she was able to relate to each child. This is the manner in which we are to relate to one another in love. Every child was special in her eyes, and she saw great possibilities in every one. The same is true of God! And the same should be true for us!

Acceptance requires grace, a lot of grace, simply because some people can be obnoxious! They test our limits. The word *patience* also comes to mind. If there was ever anyone who gave people room to be themselves, it was Jesus. He knew that the "puny" faith of the disciples would one day grow and make them into spiritual giants! What he did for them, he still does for us now. He sees who we are and how we behave, and he loves us anyway! Why? Because he knows our potential.

Yes, acceptance requires that we give each other space, but what if some people just don't change? I mean, I don't think they will ever get it! Since when were you in the people changing business? The last I knew, that was God's job! Some people are best loved with no pressure for change, at least not from us. We need to allow room for the Holy Spirit to do his thing.

Can you understand at this point why I can say, "If we cannot learn this first foundational guideline to "accept one another" then how will we ever learn to "love one another"?

Can you also see where "be devoted to one another," "live in harmony with one another," and "bear with one another" all follow and are a part of this first foundation of "accepting one another?" This is where relationships must start. This is why these are "foundational." But, there is more, much, much more, to understand if we are going to learn how to "love one another."

Part 3:

SUSTAINING GUIDELINES

The second group is the Sustaining Guidelines. This group is a little harder to bring under one word or area. They need to be dealt with separately. While there could be volumes written on each subject, I will try to explain each one briefly and simply.

It begins with perhaps the most important of the sustaining guidelines, which is to forgive one another. In Matthew 18:21–22, Peter came to Jesus and asked, "Lord, how many times shall I forgive my brother when he sins against me? Up to seven times?" Jesus answered, "I tell you, not seven times, but seventy times seven!" In Colossians 3:13, we read, "Bear with one another and *forgive* whatever grievances you may have against one another. Forgive as the Lord forgave you." One more, from Ephesians 4:30–32:

> "And do not grieve the Holy Spirit of God, with whom you were sealed for the day of redemption. Get rid of all bitterness; rage; anger and brawling and slander, along with every form

> of malice. Be kind and compassionate to one another, *forgiving* each other, just as in Christ God forgave you."

We need to remember that forgiveness is something we are called to do even when no confession or repentance has been made. Forgiveness is a manifestation of mercy, and if we forgive as Christ forgave, then we must say—as Jesus said—"Father, forgive them, for they know not what they are doing."

Forgiveness comes hard, especially in the church, because we tend to expect more from Christians. Those expectations create standards, which seem to make our failures even more inexcusable and unforgivable. This is not only true of us, but to the expectations of the world as well. Another reason is because Christians can be stubbornly self-righteous when they believe God is on their side. I point to the religious far right and far left as examples.

Offenses that require forgiveness often inflict deep wounds. These offenses create the bitterness, rage, anger, slander, and malice that Ephesians 4:31 speaks of. The pain lingers and preoccupies the mind. It leads to exhaustion and confusion and can ruin the spiritual life of even the strongest believer.

It should be noted that not all offenses require forgiveness. That's why *acceptance* comes first. All those irritating personalities, mistakes, blunders, and foolish words require *forbearance* or *acceptance* not *forgiveness.* However, when something said or done hurts us deeply and affects our fellowship, then forgiveness is in order.

Maybe we need a better understanding of what forgiveness is and what it does. For example, forgiveness does not release the offender from personal responsibility, which simply would be unjust. Forgiveness does not absolve the offender from guilt nor does it deliver the offender from the consequences, as if the law of reaping and sowing no longer applies. A Christian may have to forgive a father for abuse, for example, but that does not absolve his guilt nor take away the responsibility for his actions. That kind of cleansing only God can do! He just calls us to forgive, because it brings healing. Forgiveness has within it the power to restore relationships and cleanse away bitterness and anger. This is why it can *sustain* relationships.

Forgiveness also does not mean *forgetting.* But it helps to keep the hurts and the bitterness from suffocating the life out of relationships. It is like a growth on a tree, which envelopes a wound in the trunk. When it does this, the wound that once threatened the tree, now becomes its place of greatest strength and character. So it is with forgiveness.

In the little things, *accept.* In the big things, *forgive.* In all things, *love!*

It is said that the body has three basic needs to survive: food, water, and oxygen. But we have come to know that there is an even deeper need that goes to the depths of our very being; our soul needs God. People spend a lifetime trying to fill this need of the soul with physical things, trying to replace God. It has not worked, and it never will! However, it's not hard to see the effects of this vain attempt: strained marriages, divorce, rebellious children, violence, addictions, abuse, sickness, financial ruin, and even more. There is something fundamentally wrong with the human race, and it can be described in three letters *sin*.

As we move into the second sustaining guideline, we find the mutual command of confession and prayer. It is confession that exposes us for the sinners we are, and it is prayer that enables us to receive God's healing power. The problem we have is that confession makes us weak and vulnerable. It exposes the underside of our belly to the rest of the church. It reveals that we are not the high and mighty people we want others to think we are.

We must remember that the goal of confession is always *restoration* and not *gossip* or *rumors,* which hurt rather than heal. Healing also requires prayer. That's why the two go together as one. Praying for one another is the most powerful and effective ministry of the church, for prayer lifts us into the presence of God.

Intercessory prayer appeals to God on behalf of someone else, and it's effectiveness does not depend on how well we get along with them, how well we know them, or if we know them at all. It depends solely on God's grace and power. Therefore, prayer for one another is truly a profound act of love.

All of this is perhaps a part of serving one another. There are two words used in the Greek for the English expression "to serve." One translates "to be the slave of" and the other means "to wait on." This guideline takes on the meaning of the latter. Service begins when we are ready to give of ourselves to meet the needs of others or of the church.

Today, it seems that *time* has become our most important commodity. Whenever modern technology comes up with a new or improved invention, we are not concerned with the cost as much as "How much time will it save?" Saving time has become more important than saving money! The problem is that we have to worker harder and longer in order to pay for those "time-saving" devices. Servant hood takes time. Mowing the grass takes time. Cleaning the church takes time. Serving in the Nursery takes time. Preparing and teaching takes time. In fact, just coming to church takes time! The point is, if we find we have no time to "serve one another," then we have to take a closer look at our priorities. I ask you to think about all of the things that go into keeping a church "alive" and ask yourself if you are doing your part in the area of serving?

There is an association that most people know well called Habitat for Humanity. A group of people from all walks of life who get together and build quality homes for qualifying people. Leaders organize the project; bankers help to raise money; and carpenters, plumbers, electricians, and drywallers, and other service volunteers do what they do best. Others pack lunches, provide snacks, watch children, take pictures, and so on. Everyone is an important part of the project. The project is completed as each part does its work. Is there a message here on serving for the church?

Finally, in this section we have "encourage and build one another up!" Do you know that it is easy to be a discourager? The world is full of them: critics, negative Nellies, the can'ts and the won'ts—they are all related. I have found that it takes a lot of encouragement to make people feel good, but it only takes one word to discourage them. Encouragement is like giving someone a candy bar when they are low on energy. In the command to love one another, we must remember that love always encourages. Love always provides positive reinforcement rather than negative criticism.

Woven into the fabric of the book of Acts is the quiet yet penetrating life of a man named Barnabus. His name means "son of encouragement." His role as an encourager was an essential part in the lives of Paul and John Mark. It was Barnabus who introduced Paul to the disciples and the believers in Acts chapter eleven and encouraged their acceptance of Paul. Then, in chapter fifteen, Barnabus and Paul have a discussion about taking John Mark with them on their second journey. Paul voted against it, because John Mark had failed him once. But Barnabus believed in John Mark and insisted that he needed to be encouraged in his ministry. The outcome was that eventually John Mark became a close friend of Paul, and today, we have the Gospel of Mark as a part of our Bible, because someone encouraged him along the way.

The *call to encourage one another* is the energy that sustains rather than the criticism that drains! "You're doing a great job!" "Keep up the good work!" "We appreciate what you do to help the church!" These are words that lift and build up the body, as we encourage one another because we *love one another*.

Part 4:

CRISIS GUIDELINES

The third "one anothers" are the Crisis Guidelines. These are the ones which help get us through the hard times. Those times are when we really do need one another. There is no escape in this world from trials and tribulation. The Bible is very clear on that fact. Being a Christian does not change that fact. Everyone suffers loss, feels pain, and goes through sickness and death. We all have our disappointments, and it's during these times that we are called to bear one another's burdens and comfort one another. It's during these *crisis* situations, which we can let our light shine the brightest!

Afflictions can be both external, such as war, persecution, or mortal danger of some kind, and affliction can be internal, such as despair, anxiety, fear, or sickness. It is during these times that we find ourselves faced with all sorts of evil, doubts, fear, and questions. We cannot think about burdens or afflictions without thinking about grief. When we think about grief, we desire comfort and understanding, even if we don't verbalize it. We desire for someone to come along side and help us bear our burden and comfort us in our loss.

Crisis situations provide a special opportunity for believer's to show love in a way like no other. However, it must be said that comfort is not *pity*, and burden bearing is more than just a "hang in there!" This command involves us getting involved and putting an end to detachment and superficial cliché's.

It might even be said that only those who have committed themselves to all the former "one anothers" in the foundational and the sustaining guidelines are qualified and probably committed to follow through in the "crisis" situations. They are the ones who can truly *love* those who are hurting.

Let me explain why. The difference between comfort and burden bearing is substantial. To comfort means to stop at the side of the road and stand beside another and walk with them as they grieve, knowing in time they will recover and continue their journey of life. However, those with heavy burdens may not be able to resume their journey, unless we lift them up, carry them for a while, and eventually get them back on their feet to the point where they are able to carry their own load. You can't do that unless you have been practicing all of what it means to "love one another."

I have experienced those who must be challenged to give up the power of always being needy. They must be weaned from their dependence on others and become responsible before God. But with those, the principle problem has shifted from adversity to irresponsibility, laziness, and perhaps even disobedience. Sooner or later, we may be forced to ask the question that Jesus asked of the cripple, "Do you want to be healed?"

The final word is always one of good news, and there is one burden that we all have that no human can bear; that is the burden of sin. Jesus came to bear that burden! It was he who said, "Come unto me you who are weary, and I will give you rest" (Matthew 11:28). The only way to overcome the burden of sin is to carry that burden—no matter how great—to the foot of the cross and then to rest in the comfort and grace of God's love. He comforts us that we in turn may *comfort one another* and that we can also *carry one another's burdens.*

The final guidelines come also at a crisis time. It may be a time in the life of a believer or in the church itself. It may be a time when we "plateau" or even become stagnant. It's at these times we are called to "Spur one another on toward love and good deeds" and to "teach and admonish one another."

Believe it or not, some Christians just don't want to grow and change or become Christlike. They don't want to journey "down the narrow path." They don't want to pursue the highest and the best that Christ has to offer. They tend toward inertia. I say this because if they did, they would. But there are just too many Christians in our churches who are in this time of stagnation spiritually. It is at these times we need to spur one another on! Now, that does not mean that they need a good *kick!* It simply means we help and strongly encourage them to keep going in their walk with God. One thing we must remember is that we *spur* when not moving; we *teach and admonish* when moving in the wrong direction.

There are two ways to *spur* someone on to love and good deeds. One is through irritation and manipulation; the other is through inspiration and challenge. It is this latter kind of influence we are looking for, because it brings real change rather than resistance.

Somewhere I read a definition of *admonishment,* which says, "Wise words spoken against wrong actions." Not angry words or judgmental words, but wise words spoken in love. Our culture today does not make admonishment easy. We have exulted toleration and acceptance almost to the level of a creed. People are therefore quick to accuse their critics as being judgmental, intolerant, and insensitive when confronted about wrong actions. But, in the church, this is exactly what keeps us "in line" so to speak, when it comes to walking the "narrow road." It is exactly what is needed to keep "discord" or "dissension" from destroying our fellowship.

We are like the watchman in Ezekiel 33 who has been appointed to look after the city. If the enemy comes, we warn the city! If our warning goes unheeded, then the destruction of the city is not our fault. If, on the other hand, we fail to warn the city, then the fault for destruction is ours!

Admonishment brings out two things: confrontation and correction. That is why *teaching* is mentioned along with admonishment. Teaching appeals to the intellect, the way we think. Admonishment appeals to the way we act. Teaching deals with content, admonishment with application. Teaching sets the standard. Admonishment holds people to that standard when they have chosen to wander.

However, admonition can never be used to "clobber" someone, because they don't measure up to our expectations, but only when they don't measure up to God's! While we should *forebear* and *accept* often, we should admonish seldom. In many cases the problem may not be one of defiance or rebellion, but rather something that time and experience will correct. For example, we don't take a five year old to the doctor, because he isn't five feet tall yet! We realize it takes time to grow. But we do take him if we realize something is hindering his growth. Admonition is reserved for those times when something is hindering the natural growth of a Christian in their spiritual walk with God. It confronts the problem, teaches the truth, and attempts to correct the course. Admonishment is best done privately. Too much talk by too many people with too many opinions undermines the work of admonition.

If I may, I would like to paraphrase 2 Peter 1:3–12 in my own simple words: God has given us in his Word, and by the power of his Holy Spirit, everything we could possibly need to live the godly life of love that he desires for us. Through them we can grow and mature in an ever-increasing measure, so that we as individuals and as the church will be effective and productive through our knowledge of him.

With that in mind, let me take you back to Ephesians 4 where we first started: "As a prisoner of the Lord then, I urge you to live a life worthy of the calling you have received. Be completely humble and gentle; be patient; bearing with one another in love ... until we all reach unity in the faith and in the knowledge of the Son of God and become mature, attaining to the whole measure of the fullness of Christ. Speaking the truth in love, we will in all things grow up into him who is the head that is Christ. From him the whole body, joined and held together by every supporting ligament, grows and *builds itself up in love,* as each part does its work." Let me drive that last part home: "grows and builds itself up *in love,* as each part does its work"!

In 1 Corinthians 13, Paul said, "Now these three remain; faith, hope, and love, but the greatest of these is love"! Jesus said, "A new command I give you, love one another." Love is the most important aspect and characteristic of the body of Christ! I pray that this helps us to better understand this one supreme command of Christ to the Church. Love is the flame that brings light and warmth and life into the world. My friends, *Be Loved!*

Be Filled:

THE SPIRIT-FILLED LIFE

"Be very careful, then, how you live—not as unwise but as wise, making the most of every opportunity, because the days are evil. Therefore do not be foolish, but understand what the Lord's will is. Do not get drunk on wine, which leads to debauchery. Instead, be filled with the Spirit."

Ephesians 5:15–18

Part 1:

DOIN' THE BEST I CAN

Let's begin with this quote from Charles Stanley on the spirit-filled life: "Far too many believers think the Christian life boils down to doin' the best they can." But if that were true, then there was no need for God to send the Holy Spirit. Jesus said in John 16 (NKJV), "But it is to your advantage that I go away; for if I do not go away, the helper shall not come to you, but if I go, I will send him to you." If we don't need any help, if the Christian life is just a matter of doin' the best we can, then why send a *helper?* This was Jesus way of tipping us off to a profound truth about the Christian life. Guess what, it's impossible to attempt to live it in our power and will. The kind of life and lifestyle God has called us to as Christians is impossible to attain apart from divine intervention. And let me take that a step further; I don't believe God intended, nor does he expect, us to live it without his help. This is why Jesus said in John 15:5, "Apart from me, you can do nothing."

If there was ever a group who should have been able to live a consistent Christian walk by just doin' their best, it was the disciples. Think of all the advantages they had over you and me. They had been trained personally by Jesus himself (now, I may be a good teacher, but the greatest teacher in the world doesn't even come close!); they had seen the lame walk, the blind to see, and the dead raised to life; they had even performed a few miracles themselves. No one could have been more motivated than the disciples. Yet, in their last hours with the Master, he let them know that they were still missing something of great importance in their lives! He knew they would need more than human spirit or their own willpower and sheer determination to get the job done. So he told them to go to Jerusalem and wait for the gift.

For some Christians, the Holy Spirit is like waiting to pick someone up at the airport whom they don't know and have never seen. They desperately look for someone or something they can't possibly recognize.

Some Christians may feel that being led by the Spirit is like a slave tied to a rope is led by his master. It's kind of like the big sheep dog we used to have! When we would go for a walk, she was the master; I was the slave being pulled along! We all know we are to be led by the Spirit and filled with the Spirit, but what does that mean? And, how do we really know it's true in our own lives? This is what we are going to pursue in this chapter.

Scripture tells us that the Holy Spirit does several things in our lives; he convicts of "the guilt of sin and judgment" (John 16:8–11); he illuminates (John 16:12–15) (by the way, the term *illuminate* means "able to see; dispel darkness; or give understanding."); he teaches (John 16:12–15). As it concerns "teaching," let me interject something here; there is an old saying that "unless there is learning, there has been no teaching." The Holy Spirit can only teach the teachable. He guides (Romans 8:14); he directs (Acts 20:22). What is the difference between *guide* and *direct?* In one instance, he leads the way—that's *guide;* and in the other he points the way—that's *direct.* He assures (Romans 8:16); he intercedes (Romans 8:26); and he warns us (Acts 20:23).

The reason I bring these things to you is two-fold. First, to make sure you know these things from scripture. And second, so that when one of these things happens in your life, you will recognize the Holy Spirit. It will help increase our awareness of the Holy Spirit's "active" role in our daily lives. He was sent to assist us in all the practical matters of the Christian life. As Jesus said, he is our "helper"!

Having grown up a devout Jew, Paul had a great deal of respect for the Temple. It represented the presence of God among his people. The glory of the gospel is that because God through Christ had removed the barrier of sin, he no longer needed a building, a cloud of smoke, a pillar of fire, or a mountain top. He could take up residency in the hearts of his people through the presence of the Holy Spirit.

There is another role the Holy Spirit plays in our lives. In Ephesians 1:13, we are told that "having believed, you were marked in him with a seal, the promised Holy Spirit, who is a deposit guaranteeing our inheritance." Why do you put a *seal* on something? In those days kings and other important people of great authority wore a ring with some kind of an insignia on it that they would stamp into a wax seal on documents and letters. This would show that it was sent and was to be received with all the authority and integrity of the sender. The Holy Spirit was sent, and is to be received, with all the authority of the sender!

In Ephesians 5:15–18 it says this.

> "Be very careful, then, how you live—not as unwise, but as wise, making the most of every opportunity, because the days are evil. Therefore, do not be foolish, but understand what the Lord's will is. Do not get drunk on wine, which leads to debauchery. Instead, be filled with the Spirit."

Notice that Paul uses the terms "drunk with wine" and "filled with the Holy Spirit" together. To be drunk means more than "to drink." It means more than to be "filled up." It means to be "under the influence and control" of alcohol. It means our *mind, body, and spirit*s are all under its control. To be "filled with the Spirit" means the same thing! I see it as something that goes beyond "rededication," which amounts to us telling God that we messed up, but we will do better next time! To be filled with the Spirit requires total surrender with a realization that we can't do anything "better" without help!

Jesus said, "I have come that they may have life, and have it more abundantly." This is a two-part blessing. We cannot have the second part without the first part! We can't truly have the "abundant life" without the blessing of eternal life. Life here and now, often becomes a struggle, and we do not always see it as a blessing. However, our commitment to Christ is only the beginning; he longs to give us more. The first part of this scripture is eternal life; the second part is abundant life! This is what the Holy Spirit was sent to do in our lives. Assure us of eternal life, and help us achieve abundant life!

Again Jesus said, "I am the vine and you are the branches; if a man remains in me and I in him, he will bear much fruit; apart from Me you can do nothing." Jesus is the vine, we are the branches, and the Holy Spirit is the sap that runs through the vine giving life to the branches. The branch lives and grows and bears fruit, not by struggles and self-effort, but by simply abiding in the vine. Too often we are like branches trying to produce fruit on our own. But, Jesus' point here is that branches were not designed to *produce* fruit; they were designed to *bear* fruit!

When we try to produce the fruit of righteousness in our lives, we end up just "doin' the best we can." But when we allow the Holy Spirit to *fill us* to *totally influence and control* our body, mind, and soul; the fruit will be produced in and through us! This is the fruit of righteousness or the fruit of the Spirit, which is "love, joy, peace, patience, kindness, goodness, faithfulness, gentleness, and self-control," which we read about in Galatians, Chapter Five.

Now, let's put this together with some other scriptures:

- John 15:8: "This is to my Father's glory, that you *bear much fruit,* showing yourselves to be my disciples."

- Matthew 5:16: "In the same way, let your light shine before men, that they may see your good deeds, (*fruit*) and praise your Father in heaven."
- 2 Corinthians 9:13: "Because of the service by which you have proved yourselves, (*fruit*) men will praise God for the obedience that accompanies your confession."
- 1 Peter 2:12: "Live such good lives among the pagans that though they accuse you of doing wrong, they may see your good deeds (*fruit*) and glorify God."

The thing that all these have in common is that they are not possible without the Holy Spirit's filling us. That's why it's called the "Spirit Filled Life!"

If we are filled with the Holy Spirit, we have the potential to produce *consistent* fruit. The kind that makes even the most skeptical in life sit up and take notice. After all, the world is not attracted to the church, because we are just like they are. They are attracted because the Holy Spirit has changed and transformed us, and it's the difference that makes the difference!

The Holy Spirit took a man who made his living destroying churches and persecuting Christians (Saul) and turned him into the greatest church planter of all time (Paul)! The Holy Spirit took a group of plain, ordinary, men (the disciples) and turned them into world-class evangelists, pastors, and preachers, and it was said "that they turn the world upside down!" I'm afraid that we have stifled the work of the Holy Spirit and allowed the world to turn the church upside down!

The Christian life is certainly easier said than done, but we tend to make it harder than it is intended to be because we have not allowed ourselves to be totally under the influence of the Holy Spirit. Philippians 2:13 says, "For it is God who works in you [and me] to will and to act according to his good pleasure." God works *in* us through his Holy Spirit. It only makes sense to be *filled!*

Part 2:

WALKING BY FAITH AND KEEPING IN STEP

Remember the words of Jesus: "You shall know the truth, and the truth will set you free." This Christian life that God has called us to live in his Word, is not a matter of "doing all the right things" but a matter of "knowing the truth." The Word does not say "Be transformed by the renewing of your *will;* nor does it say *actions.* It says "by the renewing of your minds." You shall *know* the truth, and when we know the truth, it sets us free to act upon it in full confidence, because it is truth! The truth will set us free from the struggle to produce fruit and righteousness, so we can be free to *bear* fruit in our lives through faith.

Now, faith is the key that opens all of the doors of the Christian life. I think of the many scripture quotes like: "Without faith, it is impossible to please God, because anyone who comes to him must believe he exists" (Hebrews 11:6); "It is by grace you have been saved, through faith ... not by works" (Ephesians 2:8–

9); "The righteous shall live by faith" Romans 1:17); and "We live by faith and not by sight" (2 Corinthians 5:7). There are over 300 other references to the word *faith* in the New Testament alone.

1 Thessalonians 1:3 tells us that faith produces work. "We continually remember before our God and Father your work produced by faith." The works, the good deeds, our ministry to others are all prompted by our faith. It also speaks of "Your labor prompted by love"–by the way the word *labor* is interpreted "hard work," as in "giving it all we've got" or being the best we can be, because of our love (which is a fruit!)! And, he goes on to say, "your endurance inspired by hope." This is Paul's trilogy: "now these three remain; faith, hope, and love." Our faith prompts us to do; our love prompts us to do it with all our might; and our hope prompts us to see it through, until Jesus comes again!

Now our spiritual walk is not much different from a physical journey we might take. We must first believe that the place we are going exists. We also need to believe that we can get there from here! We look at a map in order to know the way, and we have faith that all these things are true … and then we go!

The same is true for the "Spirit-Filled" life. We must first believe that it exists. We must believe that we can get there from where we are. We consult the map of God's Word in order to get directions. And, if we have faith that all these things are true, we go!

The truth is that the Holy Spirit indwells within us at the point of conversion. His desire and his job is to *produce* Christlikeness in us, which is expressed or manifested through us, as we bear the fruit of the Spirit in every area of our lives.

Just like those in the Galatians church, we enter into this wonderful relationship by faith, and then for some reason, we begin conducting it by works. In Galatians 3:3, Paul says; "Are you so foolish? Having begun by the Spirit, are you now being perfected by the flesh?" If we could produce righteousness on our own, there would have been no need for the Holy Spirit. When we try to live this spiritual life and produce fruit in our own lives, we are simply trying to "improve "our flesh, which is our sinful nature. If you look up Galatians 5:16–23, you will notice the words *fruit* of the Spirit, and the *acts* of the sinful nature. We can "act," but we can't produce fruit! Only the Spirit can do that!

The Christian life is begun by faith, it runs on faith, and it ends with faith. It is lived by faith from beginning to end. So what does it mean to *walk by faith?* There is a framed quote I used to have that said; "Faith does not just believe God can, faith believes God will!"

In the story of David and Goliath, when the army of Israel saw this giant, they focused on their own ability (or inability) while David focused on God's ability! "The Lord who delivered me from the paw of the lion and the bear, he *will* deliver me from the hand of this Philistine." Not he *can,* but he *will!* That's faith.

The Christian, *Spirit-filled* life is one of knowing that when we do our part, God will produce righteous fruit in our lives. God does not expect us to struggle and try to do our best to create the Spirit-filled, fruitful life. He simply says we are to remain in the vine, and by faith, allow the life-giving, life-flowing, and fruit-producing sap of the Holy Spirit to produce the fruit, as we feed on his Word and gain understanding and grow and bloom as Christians.

As I drive down streets and roads of God's creation, I see several varieties of trees. Trees with many different colored flowers—some bloom early, some bloom late. But to the people who know what these are, we can ask, "What kind of tree is that one with the beautiful, pink blossoms"? And, they will tell us, "Oh, that's a "peach tree" or a "cheery tree" or a "Creped Myrtle." Do people recognize you by your fruit?

> "So I say, live by the Spirit, and you will not gratify the desires of the sinful nature. For the sinful nature desires what is contrary to the Spirit, and the Spirit what is contrary to the sinful nature. They are in conflict with each other, so that you do not do what you want. But if you are led by the Spirit, you are not under law. The acts of the sinful nature are obvious: sexual immorality, impurity and debauchery; idolatry and witchcraft; hatred, discord, jealousy, fits of rage, selfish ambition, dissensions, factions and envy; drunkenness, orgies, and the like. I warn you, as I did before, that those who live like this will not inherit the kingdom of God. But the fruit of the Spirit is love, joy, peace, patience, kindness, goodness, faithfulness, gentleness and self-control. Against such things there is no law. Those who belong to Christ Jesus have crucified the sinful nature with its passions and desires. *Since we live by the Spirit, let us keep in step with the Spirit.* Let us not become conceited, provoking and envying each other."
>
> Galatians 5:16–26

The Spirit filled life is a life that begins with faith, it is a walk of faith; and it ends with faith. It is a way of life that allows God to do what needs to be done in our lives in order to produce Christlikeness, as we do our part by "making every effort to add to our faith," as Paul puts it in 2 Peter 1:5. The Spirit-filled life that bears the fruit of the Spirit and is led by the Spirit is never something done through self-effort.

When the Holy Spirit came at Pentecost, there was tremendous excitement and for good reason. The focus was not only on his coming, but on the first manifestations of his coming, which were *sign*-oriented, things like speaking in tongues; healing; prophesy; and so on. The Bible does not say that after being filled with the Spirit, those in the upper room went out with great patience, kindness, gentleness, and self-control. Something supernatural had taken place, and God wanted the people to stand up and take notice! It says that they went out into the streets, speaking in tongues, and the people were "amazed and perplexed"! They asked one another "What does this mean?" We still ask that question today. Some of the people made fun of them and thought they were just drunk on wine. Then Peter suddenly stands up and begins to preach a sermon! It must have been quite a scene.

After the book of Acts, the filling of the Holy Spirit is not mentioned again with the exception of one place, in Ephesians 5:18, where Paul says, "Do not get drunk on wine, but be filled with the Holy Spirit." However, from the context of what Paul goes on to say, he is not talking about the "infilling" of the Spirit as much as the "influencing" power of the Spirit.

Allowing the Holy Spirit to totally influence or take control of our lives. So you could say that the book of Acts is all about the coming and the infilling of the Holy Spirit, while the rest of the New Testament is all about the influencing power of the Holy Spirit and how we can "keep in step" with the what the Spirit desires to do in our lives.

The shift was from sign-oriented power and gifts to character development through the influence of the Holy Spirit. Jesus never said that the Holy Spirit would come, so we could speak in tongues or do all kinds of miracles; he said that the Holy Spirit would come to "convict the world of the guilt of sin" and teach about righteousness and judgment.

The Bible also says that there is a definite and important relationship between our thinking and our ability to follow the Spirit. It says "those who walk according to the flesh have their *minds set* on the things of the flesh but, those who live according to the Spirit have their *minds set* on what the Spirit desires." Romans 8:5–6 tells us, "Set your *minds* on things above not on things of the earth." Colossians 3:2 says "Whatever is true, whatever is honorable, right, pure, lovely, of good repute, anything of excellence, or worthy of praise, *think* on these things." (In order to live the Spirit filled life we must have our minds–our thinking–focused on what the Spirit desires and allow him to produce those things in our life!

Let's go back to the vine illustration. The only real evidence that the branch is actually abiding in the vine is the presence or the absence of fruit. It is amazing how often we are prone to substitute other measures or standards as to whether or not a person is walking with God. For some, all it takes is to hear the words "I'm a Christian." Others would say they can tell by the way you dress or don't dress. Some would say they know, because you attend church or because you are a Sunday school teacher. But God's standard is fruit!

The two most popular substitutes for fruit are gifts and talent. While all of these are certainly part of the life of a Christian, they are all easily faked! They can all be produced by self-effort! I say, "Look for the fruit—not perfection—for we all have faults, but the character fruit of "love, joy, peace, patience, kindness, goodness, faithfulness, gentleness, and especially, self-control."

Let's look at Matthew 7:15–23:

> "Watch out for false prophets. They come to you in sheep's clothing, but inwardly they are ferocious wolves. *By their fruit you will recognize them.* Do people pick grapes from thorn bushes, or figs from thistles? Likewise every good tree bears good fruit, but a bad tree bears bad fruit. A good tree cannot bear bad fruit, and a bad tree cannot bear good fruit. Every tree that does not bear good fruit is cut down and thrown into the fire. Thus, *by their fruit you will recognize them.*
>
> Not everyone who says to Me, 'Lord, Lord,' will enter the kingdom of heaven, but only he who does the will of my Father who is in heaven. Many will say to me on that day, 'Lord, Lord, did we not prophesy in your name, and in your name drive out demons and perform many miracles?' Then I will tell them plainly, '*I never knew you.* Away from me, you evildoers!"

Twice he says "by their fruit you will recognize them." And then he goes on to mention some works and some gifts: "prophecy," "cast out demons," and "perform miracles," and he declares "away from me ... I never knew you!" It's like he is asking, "Where's the fruit?"

One last thing I want to mention is this: we all know that the Ten Commandments are relational and are summed up in the commands to "Love the Lord your God with all your heart, mind, soul, and strength; and love your neighbor as yourself." Well, the fruit of the Spirit is relational as well; the first three, love, joy, and peace, relate to God and come only through the indwelling Holy Spirit. The next three, patience, kindness, and goodness, concern our relationship with one another and can only be produced by abiding in the vine—again by the Holy Spirit. The last three, faithfulness, gentleness, and self-control, relate to self, and also can only be produced by the influencing power of the Holy Spirit changing our will. If we are truly "Spirit-filled" Christians, we will bear the fruit of those things in which we are strong and the Spirit has produced in us, and we will work with the Holy Spirit in the areas we are weak and still need improvement. That's what it means to "keep in step" with the Holy Spirit.

Part 3:

STAYING BETWEEN THE BUOYS

"If you love Me, you will obey what I command. And I will ask the Father, and He will give you another Counselor to be with you forever—the Spirit of truth. The world cannot accept Him, because it neither sees him nor knows him. But you know him, for He lives with you and will be in you ... All this I have spoken while still with you. But the Counselor, the Holy Spirit, whom the Father will send in My name, will teach you all things and will remind you of everything I have said to you ... "Now I am going to him who sent me, yet none of you asks me, 'Where are you going?' Because I have said these things, you are filled with grief. But I tell you the truth: It is for your good that I am going away. Unless I go away, the Counselor will not come to you; but if I go, I will send him to you. When He comes, He will convict the world of guilt in regard to sin and righteousness and judgment: in regard to sin, because men do not believe in me; in regard to righteousness, because I am going to the Father,

> where you can see me no longer; and in regard to judgment, because the prince of this world now stands condemned. I have much more to say to you, more than you can now bear. But when He, the Spirit of truth, comes, He will guide you into all truth. He will not speak on His own; He will speak only what He hears, and He will tell you what is yet to come. He will bring glory to me by taking from what is mine and making it known to you."
>
> John 14:15–17

I want to start with an illustration to get our focus in the right direction. For several years my three sons and I have fished for walleye on the St. Louis River, which flows into Lake Superior in Wisconsin. It's the only place I know where we can always catch fish. We have never been "skunked." The first time my sons and I were going up river, we were given advice to make sure we stayed between the buoys. You see, all along the river there are marker buoys—green on one side and red on the other. As long as you stay between the buoys, you are in the channel. But if you strayed off course at all, you would soon find yourself in about two feet of water and quickly beach the boat.

One of the primary roles of the Holy Spirit is that of a *guide.* I think that as our guide the Holy Spirit also gives us some spiritual markers that guide us along the "narrow way" and keep us from running aground in life.

I do not believe that God is a God of confusion. I especially don't think he wants us to be confused about his will and his plan for our lives. So I want to look at three spiritual markers that we can always count on to guide us in the Spirit filled life. The emphasis is on the word "guide," because the Holy Spirit does not control us, or force us, or push us to do anything. Jesus said he would "guide" us. If we choose to follow his guidance, he will keep us between the buoys.

Marker number one is the marker of "peace." The *presence* or *absence* of peace is often the first indicator that the Holy Spirit is up to something, and we should heed his guidance. Inner peace is a hard concept to define. Even the Word says it's a peace that "passes all understanding." However, it is not hard at all to recognize its absence! Let's look at that scripture found in Philippians 4:6–7. "Do not be anxious about anything, but in everything, by prayer and petition, with thanksgiving, present your requests to God. And the peace of God, which transcends all understanding, will guard your hearts and your minds in Christ Jesus."

If I may paraphrase this in my own words, I would say pray and call upon God for all your requests, decisions, and concerns, and before your prayers are even answered, there will be a peace from God that will tell you that you are on the right track. I can't explain it, it's beyond our understanding, but it's there. And if it's not there, you might be out of the channel! Beware, lest you beach the boat! Paul says that this peace will "guard our hearts and minds." This is very important because our hearts and minds control our *actions!* Whether we are talking about good actions or bad, this is always the cycle: It begins with a thought in our mind; the more we think about it, it soon stirs one of many emotions in our heart; and if the emotion is strong enough, it soon becomes an action! Again, the cycle is the same, good or bad.

Now, as much as God loves us and wants to keep us out of trouble, he will not violate our freewill and force us to do the right thing or make the right decision. But that's exactly why it's so important to develop sensitivity to the presence or the absence of God's peace in our lives.

Marker number two is the marker of conscience. In some ways you could say that it is our conscience that provides the presence or absence of peace. We have all heard the old saying; "Let your conscience be your guide" and, as Christians, that's exactly what we should do. God has placed within us a moral barometer, an inner capacity that is constantly accusing or defending motives and actions. Within my computer, there is basic standard code for everything. Every program has its own code. If I do something that is contrary to that code, a little box comes up on the screen and tells me I have done something wrong! Or, it will ask, "Do you really want to do this?" When we become Christians, I believe the Holy Spirit resets God's original standard code for life, and he begins reprogramming our conscience and renewing our minds to more specific and complete truths that reflect God's code! When we are tempted, our conscience says "Do you really want to do this?"

Marker number three is the Word of God itself. Again, 1 Peter 1:3 tells us that "his divine power has given us everything we need for life and godliness." It is the inerrant, infallible, and inspired Word of God. 2 Peter 1:20 tells us that "no prophesy of scripture is a matter of one's own interpretation, but men—moved by the Holy Spirit—spoke from God." In light of what we read from John 16:13, this makes perfect sense. Jesus said that the Holy Spirit "would not speak on his own, he will speak only what he hears. He will take from what is mine and make it known to you." That's how we received God's Word. Through those who wrote down the things that the Holy Spirit "made known to them." It is the work of the Holy Spirit to bring thoughts to our minds, remind us of truth, and point us in the direction of truth from God's Word. But we need to be constantly aware of his presence. The Spirit-filled life is a life that stays between the markers of peace, conscience, and God's Word; it's what Jesus called the "narrow way."

Part 4

THE POWER OF FRUIT

The Fruit of the Spirit is:

Love, Joy, and Peace: (Relating to God)

Patience, Kindness, and Goodness: (Relating to Man)

Faithfulness, Gentleness, and Self-Control: (Relating to Self)

I want to look a little closer at the relationship between the power of God and the fruit of the Spirit. What do you think of when I mention the "power of God?" Normally, our minds are catapulted into the realm of the spectacular: healings, miracles, the resurrection, and the like. However, the power of the Holy Spirit was given for the express purpose of enabling believers to be effective witnesses. Acts 1:8 says, "But you will receive *power* when the Holy Spirit comes on you; and *you will be my witnesses* in Jerusalem, and in all Judea and Samaria, and to the ends of the earth."

When we look at the fruit of the Spirit, we would think that it is meant to make us holy and righteous, or at the very least, a good person. That is a nice byproduct, but there is more to it than that. The fruit of the Spirit is one of two channels through which God releases his power in us and through us. The other is through the *gifts* of the Spirit. These enable us to be his witnesses in three ways:

1. The fruit and the gifts attract non-believers to the body of Christ.
2. The fruit and the gifts provide the qualities needed to enable the body of Christ to work in harmony.
3. The fruit and the gifts protect us from the destructive consequences of sin.

The most powerful sermon in the world is no match for the power of a Spirit-filled life. Why? Because non-believers are not as impressed with what Christians believe, what they preach or what they know; as they are with how Christians act.

These two channels through which God works are really intertwined. It's the relational qualities of the fruit, which allow the body to work together successfully. In a sense, the fruit of the Spirit functions like the oil in an engine. Without oil, the friction between the parts of an engine causes the parts to eventually destroy each other, and the engine soon comes to a grinding halt. Just as the members of a physical body work interdependently with one another to accomplish the will of the brain, so the members of Christ's body are to work together to accomplish God's will.

The Spirit's fruit of love, joy, and peace are produced in us as our relationship with God grows deeper, first, through our worship and second, through our study. We study God's Word in order to get to know him. I mean to really *know* him, to know his character; his wisdom; and his holiness. Then the things we come to know, lead us to worship. And, our worship leads us to desire to know him better, which leads to a deeper worship, and on it goes. It is our worship created through the power of love, joy, and peace that invites others to want to know this God that has transformed our life!

The Spirit's fruit of patience, kindness, and goodness are produced in us also for a two-fold reason: That we might get along with and work in harmony with one another. And, that this in turn would draw others into the fellowship. Think of it in terms of a family. We call ourselves the family of God, so what kind of family would you desire to be a part of? One where there is always quarreling and friction and distrust and selfishness, and little love or caring? Or a family where people care about one-another and love one another and have patience with each other and a desire to work all things for the benefit and harmony of the family?

Finally, when you and I allow the Holy Spirit to produce in us the rare values of faithfulness, gentleness, and self-control, we are in a sense allowing him to provide us with a powerful, defense system. These are the qualities we need the most when temptation and trial comes knocking on our door. These can never be consistent, if we try to produce them. But they will always be consistent if they are produced by the Holy Spirit.

"His divine power has given us everything we need for life and godliness through our knowledge of Him who called us by His own glory and goodness. Through these He has given us his very great and precious promises, so that through them you may participate in the divine nature and *escape the corruption in the world caused by evil desires.* For this very reason, make every effort to add to your faith goodness; and to goodness, knowledge; and to knowledge, self-control; and to self-control, perseverance; and to perseverance, godliness; and to godliness, brotherly kindness; and to brotherly kindness, love. For if you possess these qualities in *increasing measure,* they will *keep you from being ineffective and unproductive* in your knowledge of our Lord Jesus Christ. But if anyone does not have them, he is nearsighted and blind, and has forgotten that he has been cleansed from his past sins.

Therefore, my brothers, be all the more eager to make your calling and election sure. For if you do these things, *you will never fall,* and you will receive a rich welcome into the eternal kingdom of our Lord and Savior Jesus Christ. So I will always remind you of these things, even though you know them and are firmly established in the truth you now have."

2 Peter 1:3–11

It's the power of fruit!

Part 5:

THE SPIRIT AT WORK IN GOD'S PEOPLE

When Jesus died on the cross and rose from the dead, Satan was condemned and the world was redeemed. Jesus freed us not only from the condemnation of sin, but from the power of sin. There are three ways the Holy Spirit works in the world that all point to the cross. (1) convicting of the guilt of sin because of unbelief, (2) convicting of righteousness, because Jesus was going to the Father where they could see him no more, and (3) convicting of judgment, a judgment that has already taken place, and one to come.

The Holy Spirit also works in God's people, leading them to become a force of change and a deterrent of evil. The three main areas he works in the church are direction, protection, and edification." These are only as effective as the church allows them to be.

There are five areas given to us in scripture where the Holy Spirit works in or with believers. It says, he will "teach us all things" and he will "remind us of the things Jesus said", he will help us pray, will help us witness, and in and through all these areas, helps us to become Christlike.

Two of these are given in John 14:26, "The Counselor, the Holy Spirit, whom the Father will send in my name, will teach you all things and will remind you of everything I have said to you." These are the two areas of our Christian life where the Holy Spirit works to bring us *understanding.* Without the insightful teaching of the Holy Spirit, we would never understand God's Word. Of course this can only happen when we are leading a Spirit-filled life. Even though a gifted teacher or preacher may be explaining truth from God's Word, unless the Holy Spirit bears witness to that truth in our hearts, we will not truly understand. The scripture, "The man without the Spirit does not accept the things that come from the Spirit of God, for they are foolishness to him" (1 Corinthians 2:14), applies to people in the church as well! John 12:16 says, "At first his disciples did not understand all this. Only after Jesus was glorified did they realize that these things had been written about him." All the while Jesus was teaching them and explaining the scripture to them, they were clueless! John 2:22 says, "After he was raised from the dead, his disciples recalled what he had said. Then they believed the scripture and the words that Jesus had spoken."

The Holy Spirit helped them piece the puzzle together by bringing to their remembrance the things Jesus did and said. And, once they "got it," the Holy Spirit helped them to proclaim it!

Romans 8:26 says, "Likewise the Spirit also helps us in our weaknesses. For we do not know what we should pray for as we ought, but the Spirit himself makes intercession for us." I have learned over the years that I can pray, knowing that the love of God wants the best for me. The wisdom of God knows what is best for me. And, the power of God can accomplish it.

The Spirit is the master translator of our thoughts, desires, and needs into language that the Father completely understands. The Spirit is not dependent upon our vocabulary, our diction, or our theological understanding to present our heart felt needs before the throne of grace. Praise God that we can come boldly to the throne of grace "so that we might receive mercy and find grace to help us in our time of need" (Hebrews 4:16). Listen, when we want to pray and don't know where to begin, God already sees what is on our heart.

The Spirit also helps believers witness. In this there are three main areas that the Spirit of God concentrates on: *words, life, and deeds.* Some people are gifted in the use of words, verbalizing their witness for Christ. But some have a harder time in this area. However, witnessing is far more than just telling people about Christ. It's about living the life of Christ before them. It is a much more powerful witness when lifestyle backs up words. The very name *Christian* was coined by non-believers, as they observed the lifestyle of the early followers. Unfortunately, the church struggles in this area today.

There is a place for deeds. But even our deeds can have an adverse effect if done in the wrong spirit, motive, or attitude. If we will allow him, and if we ask him, the Holy Spirit will help us in all of these areas to be an *affective* witness for the Lord.

The primary work of the Holy Spirit in the

believer is to conform us into the likeness of Christ. We should never lose sight of that fact. The desire to be Christlike does not create the reality. We cannot "imitate" Christ. Christlikeness comes from the inside out. What a great blessing it is when we realize the work of the Holy Spirit on our behalf! We need his indwelling; we need his empowering; and most of all we need his presence in our lives. We must be *Spirit-Filled!*

Part 6:

DISCOVERING SPIRITUAL GIFTS

Let me begin by explaining the difference between spiritual gifts and the fruit of the Spirit. As Christians, our spiritual gifts define what we do, while the fruit of the Spirit defines what we are. The fruit of the Spirit is like an orange; all the sections of "peace, joy, patience, kindness, goodness, faithfulness, gentleness, and self-control" are all wrapped up in the rind of "love," which holds it all together. That's why it doesn't say *fruits* (plural). Let me paraphrase what Paul says in 1 Corinthians 13: I could have all of the gifts listed in the New Testament, but if I have not (the fruit of the Spirit) *love*—I am just a clanging cymbal! Sometimes I think, to the world, the church is like the *Gong Show.* We can show off all we want, but if we lack love, it is all for naught.

As it concerns spiritual gifts, we will discover that we may have a general gift with a specific calling. For instance; a person with the gift of teaching (general) may be called to use that gift among children, or another might be called to teach an adult study or yet another to teach through the venue of books or tapes. One might be given the gift of missions (general) and be called to Zambia or Chicago, or just to be the missions leader in a local church. The point is that within each general gift there are many specific ways God may assign that gift to be used.

Spiritual gifts are not designed for "lone rangers." Each of the three major references to spiritual gifts in the Bible also mentions the *body* of Christ. God has chosen to make the body a living organism, with Jesus as the head and each member functioning with one or more gifts to keep it alive and growing and functioning properly. Romans 12:4–8 tells us,

> "Just as each of us has one body with many members, and these members do not all have the same function, so in Christ we who are many form one body, and each member belongs to all the others. We have different gifts, according to the grace given us. If a man's gift is prophesying, let him use it in proportion to his faith. If it is serving, let him serve; if it is teaching, let him teach; if it is encouraging, let him encourage; if it is contributing to the needs of others, let him give generously; if it is leadership, let him govern diligently; if it is showing mercy, let him do it cheerfully."

Ephesians 4:16 says "from Him (that is Christ) the whole body, joined and held together by every supporting ligament, grows and builds itself up in *love* as each part does it's work." 1 Corinthians 12:26 reads this way, "If one part suffers, every part suffers with it; if one part is honored, every part rejoices with it." I like to think in terms of: if one part is not working like it should, we all suffer! In light of this, how important is it that we discover and develop our spiritual gifts?

Notice that as I put this chapter together I listed *discover* before *develop*. That's because no one can decide what gift they would like to have and then develop it! In other words, I can't decide I want to have the gift of teaching; God gives the gift! We must first discover what that gift is, and then there are two ways we develop that gift. One is through knowledge; the other is through experience, which is the practice of our knowledge!

When you think about the human body and how it functions, you find that we have two eyes, two ears, two hands, ten fingers and ten toes, thirty-six teeth, two kidneys, one heart, and so on. What does this tell us concerning the *gifts* the "many parts" of the church? Well, it tells me that we do not all have the same function, and that there may be more than one person with the same gift. But it takes them all doing their part for the church to be alive and healthy. The obvious action to take then would be to work together to accomplish what needs to be done! If there are several with the gift of teaching, they don't try to outdo each other, nor do they waste their time comparing themselves to one another. They are to work together to get the job done and glorify God!

That being said, we need to know that our spiritual giftedness is not just something we do; it is a part of who we are. Our spiritual gift is inclusive of our talents, our experience, our skills, our knowledge and our passion—all of which *develop* our giftedness. Through our knowledge we come to experience; through experience we develop our skills and talents. It's our knowledge and experience working together that develops a passion for what we enjoy doing the most. All of these lead us to our spiritual gift. It is what Rick Warren, author of *The Purpose Driven Life,* calls our "S.H.A.P.E." I and others have found true blessing in using our spiritual giftedness in and through the church–the body of Christ–which brings glory to God! In that there is great reward!

> "Now about spiritual gifts, brothers, I do not want you to be ignorant. There are different kinds of gifts, but the same Spirit. There are different kinds of service, but the same Lord. There are different kinds of working, but the same God works all of them in all men. Now to each one the manifestation of the Spirit is given for the common good. To one there is given through the Spirit the message of wisdom, to another the message of knowledge by means of the same Spirit, to another faith by the same Spirit, to another gifts of healing by that one Spirit, to another miraculous powers, to another prophecy, to another distinguishing between spirits, to another speaking in different kinds of tongues, and to still another the interpretation of tongues. All these are the work of one and the same Spirit, and He gives them to each one, just as He determines. The body is a unit, though it is made up of many parts; and though all its parts are many, they form one body. So it is with Christ. For we were all baptized by one Spirit into one body, whether Jews or Greeks, slave or free—and we

were all given the one Spirit to drink. Now the body is not made up of one part but of many. If the foot should say, "Because I am not a hand, I do not belong to the body," it would not for that reason cease to be part of the body. And if the ear should say, "Because I am not an eye, I do not belong to the body," it would not for that reason cease to be part of the body. If the whole body were an eye, where would the sense of hearing be? If the whole body were an ear, where would the sense of smell be? But in fact God has arranged the parts in the body, every one of them, just as he wanted them to be. If they were all one part, where would the body be? As it is, there are many parts, but one body. The eye cannot say to the hand, "I don't need you!" And the head cannot say to the feet, "I don't need you!" On the contrary, those parts of the body that seem to be weaker are indispensable, and the parts that we think are less honorable we treat with special honor. And the parts that are unpresentable are treated with special modesty, while our presentable parts need no special treatment. But God has combined the members of the body and has given greater honor to the parts that lacked it, so that there should be no division in the body, but that its parts should have equal concern for each other. If one part suffers, every part suffers with it; if one part is honored, every part rejoices with it.

Now you are the body of Christ, and each one of you is a part of it. And in the church God has appointed first of all apostles, second prophets, third teachers, then workers of miracles, also

> those having gifts of healing, those able to help others, those with gifts of administration, and those speaking in different kinds of tongues. Are all apostles? Are all prophets? Are all teachers? Do all work miracles? Do all have gifts of healing? Do all speak in tongues? Do all interpret? But eagerly desire the greater gifts. And now I will show you the most excellent way."
>
> 1 Corinthians 12

And he goes on to write about *love,* because without love the gifts are useless.

Let's set the context. The Corinthian church was beset with many problems and difficulties. The church was filled with division, arguments, lawsuits, and immorality. On top of all that, there was confusion about marriage, food sacrificed to idols, worship, the Lord's Supper, the resurrection, giving, and spiritual gifts. We must remember that the church was really very young. When Paul wrote his letters to this church, he specifically addressed all of these issues. In chapter twelve, he addresses the issue of spiritual gifts. In this scripture, I find six directives to help them and us understand better.

He says in verse one, "I do not want you to be ignorant." I think this not only means ignorant of what our gift is, but also how and why our giftedness is too be used. In verses four through six, he uses the word *different* three times, meaning "different gifts," "different service," and "different workings." There are about twenty gifts given in the Bible. They are found in Romans 12, 1 Corinthians 12, Ephesians 4, and 1

Peter 4:10–11. Some Bible scholars will categorize the gifts this way:

- Speaking gifts: Word of wisdom, prophecy, evangelism, pastor, and teacher.
- Service gifts: Administration, exhortation, faith, giving, helps, serving, and mercy.
- Sign gifts: Distinguishing spirits, miracles, healing, tongues, and interpretation of tongues.

In verses seven through eleven, he talks about the distribution of gifts: "All these are the work of one and the same Spirit, and he gives them to each one, just as he determines." It's important to know that we are all expected to do many of the things listed as *spiritual gifts.* For example, while some may have the gift of giving, we are all to be givers of our resources for kingdom purposes. Likewise, we are not excused from witnessing, just because we may not have the gift of evangelism.

In verses fourteen through twenty, we are reminded that the body is made up of many different parts having a variety of uses. "But in fact God has arranged the parts in the body, every one of them, just as he wanted them to be. If they were all one part, where would the body be? As it is, there are many parts, but one body."

We are all given a spiritual gift. In verse seven, he says, "Now to *each one* the manifestation of the Spirit is given for the common good." He gives them to each one, and that gift needs to be identified and used for God's glory!

Every gift is important for the *body* to stay healthy and active and performing properly. Verse twenty-six says, "If one part suffers, every part suffers with it; if one part is honored, every part rejoices with it."

If we understand these directives, we will better understand the *gifts* of the Spirit. Let me give you some steps to *discovering and developing* your spiritual giftedness.

The first step is to believe that God has gifted you and has an assignment for you to accomplish in the body of Christ. If you are serious, and willing to use your gifts for his glory and the benefit of the body of Christ, God will help you discover and develop that assignment. Like Paul, God does not want you to remain "ignorant."

The second step is to explore the possibilities. This usually starts with taking a "spiritual gifts" test of some kind. There are several available. This allows you to use your creative imagination to fit the "square peg in the right hole" so to speak. God will lead you to something you will enjoy doing; even if you have never done it before, if it is your gift it will also become your passion! It will also normally fit your knowledge, skills, and experience in life.

The third step is to pray. Pray that God will lead the way. Pray that God will ignite the spark within your heart and show you a real passion. Pray for opportunities (and not opposition) within the body of Christ.

The fourth step is to be *trained and equipped* to serve. In other words, we need to seek out anything that may help us in our area of giftedness. It may be books, seminars, schooling, tapes, or even people who have had success doing whatever it is you desire to do.

Step five is to expect confirmation. People will respond to your gift, and they will also confirm your gift through compliments and encouragement. There is a quote that I remember that says, "If you think you are a leader and have the gift of leadership and no one is following, you are just a guy taking a walk!" Our gifts will always be confirmed.

Step six is expect affirmation from God. This means that God will bless our service to him, and we will "bear much fruit!" God will open doors we didn't even know were there!

Step seven: don't put it off!

Part 7:

DEVELOPING YOUR GIFTS

Today we live in an electronic world, with ever-increasing technology. The computer I have in my study has far more power than computers that filled up an entire room in the 1960's. It contains more information on its hard drive than all the books on my bookshelves combined. As powerful as it is, it will be nothing more than a doorstop in a couple of years and probably extinct in another five or six. But for now it serves my purpose and more. There is only one problem however. With all the time, effort, manpower, and money that went into it, it's absolutely worthless unless it is connected to a source of power.

In the same way, a Christian, even with all the right gifts, experience, talents, and abilities—even plugged into the right place of service—is not going to be effective unless he or she is connected with the power source of the Spirit of God. For our service to have power and effectiveness, God must be working through us!

- John 7:38–39: "Whoever believes in Me, as the scripture has said, steams of living water will flow from within him." By this *he meant the Spirit* whom those who believed in him were later to receive."
- Luke 24:49: "I am going to send you what my Father has promised; but stay in the city until you have been *clothed with power* from on high."
- Acts 1:8: "But you will *receive power* when the Holy Spirit comes upon you; and you will be my witnesses."
- John 15:4–5: "No branch can bear fruit by itself; it must remain in the vine. Neither can you bear fruit unless you remain in me. I am the vine; you are the branches. If a man remains in me and I in him, he will bear much fruit; *apart from me you can do nothing*."

Our most often prayed prayer ought to be: "Lord, don't let me be satisfied with what I can do for you, but allow me to see what only you can do through me." In his words, "apart from me you can do nothing," there are two ways Jesus could have said "nothing" in the Greek. The one he chose to have written means "not even one thing." I have seen people do a lot of things without him—even religious things—and good things, but I have not seen people doing eternal things without him! Using the analogy of John 15, what he seems to be saying is, you might be able to make artificial branches and leaves, but you can't make grapes not even one. Apart from the indwelling, empowering work of God, we cannot produce *fruit!*

In Ephesians 5:18, Paul commands us to be "filled with the Spirit," not for just a moment, but as a way of life. I have met many people who claim to be filled with the Spirit, but their everyday lives cause me to think they have pretty shallow tanks! To be filled with the Spirit is not like filling an empty glass with water! We got all the Spirit we are going to get when we became Christians. The issue is not about getting more of the Spirit; it is all about the Spirit getting more of us!

According to the scripture, there are three things we do that prevents us from being filled. The first is in Acts 7:51: "Do not resist." Resistance can be because of rebellion, it can be a "Lackawanna," or just ignorance, which is not knowing or refusing to seek what God is doing or wants to do in our lives.

The second is Ephesians 4:30–32: "Do not grieve the Holy Spirit." We grieve the Holy Spirit when we say or do anything that is not God's will. In a word, it's called *sin.* It also grieves the Holy Spirit when we cause disunity and dissension in the body of Christ. I also have to think the Holy Spirit is grieved when we do not use the gifts he has given us to their fullest potential.

The third is in 1 Thessalonians 5:19: "Do not put out the Spirit's fire," refusing to step out in faith and trust him or allow him to move and work in our midst. To "stifle" the work of God in and through the church or his people will put out the Spirit's fire!

The key to power serving is "surrender." It is in saying to God,

> I can't, but you can! I can teach, but only you Lord can change lives. I can give, but only you Lord can empower my gift! I can sing, but only you Lord can move hearts to repentance and stir emotions to surrender. I can serve in many ways with the giftedness you have given, but only you Lord, can save!

The power of every gift is not in the gift itself, it's not in the user, but it is in the giver! Apart from him, we cannot do a single thing of eternal value or significance.

As one of my former teachers used to say, "I said all that to say this ... " All of these things will prevent us from developing our gifts. We need to be filled with the Spirit, we must not resist what he wants to do through us to serve others, and we must know that he is grieved when we do not develop our gifts. All of these will "put out the Spirit's fire" in any church. These are the reasons why ten percent of the people do all the work!

I have used a great resource from a book by Christian A. Schwarz called *Natural Church Development,* which illustrates this point perfectly. He shows a picture of a wagon—representing the church—being pushed and pulled by two men straining for all they are worth. The problem is that the wagon has square wheels, while all the time it is filled with round wheels! [22]

That being said, there is also nothing more frustrating than long term service in an area where you are not gifted. We need to recognize where God has gifted us for sure. We need to make the decision to discover, develop, and use our gifts wherever they are needed. But we also need to know where we are *not* gifted. Doing something we are not gifted to do can be just as big of a barrier to growth and fruitfulness as anything else in the church, as well as to us individually. We must discover and develop that which God has gifted us to do and do it all for his glory and honor, not ours!

Living Life from the Overflow:

BLESSED TO BE A BLESSING

"Now he who supplies seed to the sower and bread for food will also supply and increase your store of seed and will enlarge the harvest of your righteousness. You will be made rich in every way so that you can be generous on every occasion, and through us your generosity will result in thanksgiving to God. This service that you perform is not only supplying the needs of God's people but is also *overflowing* in many expressions of thanks to God. Because of the service by which you have proved yourselves, men will praise God for the obedience that accompanies your confession of the gospel of Christ, and for your generosity in sharing with them and with everyone else. And in their prayers for you their hearts will go out to you, because of the surpassing grace God has given you. Thanks be to God for his indescribable gift!"

2 Corinthians 9:10–13

"Give, and it will be given to you. A good measure, pressed down, shaken together and *running over,* will be poured into your lap. For with the measure you use, it will be measured to you."

Luke 6:38

"Bring the whole tithe into the storehouse, that there may be food in my house. Test me in this," says the LORD Almighty, "and see if I will not throw open the floodgates of heaven and *pour out so much blessing that you will not have room enough for it.*"

Malachi 3:10

"So then, just as you received Christ Jesus as Lord, continue to live in him, rooted and built up in him, strengthened in the faith as you were taught, and *overflowing with thankfulness.*"

Colossians 2:7

"May the Lord make your love increase and *overflow* for each other and for everyone else, just as ours does for you."

1 Thessalonians 3:12

"May the God of hope fill you with all joy and peace as you trust in Him, so that you may *overflow with hope* by the power of the Holy Spirit."

Romans 15:13

Jesus answered, "Everyone who drinks this water will be thirsty again, but whoever drinks the water I give him will never thirst. Indeed, the water I give him will become in him a *spring of water welling up to eternal life.*"

John 4:13

"On the last and greatest day of the Feast, Jesus stood and said in a loud voice, "If anyone is thirsty, let him come to me and drink. Whoever believes in me, as the Scripture has said, *streams of living water will flow from within him.*"

John 7:38

Part 1:

FILLED TO OVERFLOWING

"If you fully obey the LORD your God and carefully follow all his commands I give you today, the LORD your God will set you high above all the nations on earth. *All these blessings will come upon you and accompany you* if you obey the LORD your God:

You will be blessed in the city and blessed in the country.

The fruit of your womb will be blessed, and the crops of your land and the young of your livestock—the calves of your herds and the lambs of your flocks.

Your basket and your kneading trough will be blessed.

You will be blessed when you come in and blessed when you go out.

The LORD will grant that the enemies who rise up against you will be defeated before you. They will come at you from one direction but flee from you in seven.

The LORD will send a blessing on your barns and on everything you put your hand to. The LORD your God will bless you in the land he is giving you.

The LORD will establish you as his holy people, as he promised you on oath, if you keep the commands of the LORD your God and walk in his ways. Then all the peoples on earth will see that you are called by the name of the LORD, and they will fear you.

The LORD will grant you abundant prosperity—in the fruit of your womb, the young of your livestock and the crops of your ground—in the land he swore to your forefathers to give you.

The LORD will open the heavens, the storehouse of his bounty, to send rain on your land in season and to bless all the work of your hands. You will lend to many nations but will borrow from none.

The LORD will make you the head, not the tail. If you pay attention to the commands of the LORD your God that I give you this day and carefully follow them, you will always be at the top, never at the bottom."

Deuteronomy 28:1–13

Now, that is a list of blessings!

But, there's more. Please reread the scripture for this chapter. How do you feel about these scriptures?

Do you believe that God desires to bless you, your church, this nation, or this world in ways such as these? The chapter title, "Living Life from the Overflow," is more than just a title; it is more than a concept; it is a lifestyle! It is a vision and a desire of God for the church. More specifically, I believe this is a vision God has for you!

What kinds of thoughts or pictures did you see or hear or feel or think as you read those scriptures? My mind was saturated with thoughts like: blessings, abundance, and generosity—so much it is overflowing!

I was driving down the highway one day and I saw an old motel. The sign said that it was called The Fountain. As I drove by, I could see a place where it looked like there may have been a fountain at one time. It may have looked much like the picture at the beginning of this chapter. The problem is that I never have seen the fountain! The fountain is no longer there. Now, I have no idea what this motel was like in the past or what it is like now. In fact, I don't even know if it is still a motel! But one thing I do know is that there is something profoundly unsettling about a dried up fountain. Something that is supposed to flow with life and spew in the air, splash, and overflow becomes a picture of death, sadness, and emptiness, which you know just doesn't belong there.

What if the Christian life was like a fountain? I mean, what if love, joy, hope, and peace, just flowed from deep within and spewed up and splashed down and just overflowed with the abundance and the blessings that these scriptures talk about? How refreshing! How captivating! How wonderful that would be!

In John 10:10, Jesus said; "The thief comes only

to steal and kill and destroy; I have come that they may have life, and have it to the full." Another translation says "and have it more abundantly." Now, if you look up the word *abundant* you would find words like "ample, rich, lavish, generous, plentiful, bountiful, and *overflowing!*" Of course!

The thief is subtle and devious, and he wants to rob us of every drop of whatever is "true, honorable, right, pure, lovely, admirable, excellent or praiseworthy" in life (Philippians 4:8). But the good news is that Jesus came that we might have an "overflowing" life, overflowing with an abundance of all these things!

If your kids have ever left the water running in the bathtub or the toilet has ever overflowed, you know what an *abundant* amount of water all over the floor is like! But what does an overflowing life look like? In my mind, it looks like the fountain in the picture.

Every Sunday in our church we would sing the Doxology: "Praise God from whom all blessings flow." Do we really mean it? Do we really believe it? Where does our joy come from? Where does our peace come from? According to all these scriptures, our blessings come from God, and we are created to be a channel, through which, his blessings can flow. God said to Abraham, "All nations will be blessed by you." He was blessed to be a blessing! God wants to fills us and continue to fill us with the life giving water of the Holy Spirit, so we will spill over into the lives of others.

The central column of the fountain is where the never-ending supply of life-giving water bubbles up and fills the first bowl—that's *you!* Then it overflows into the second bowl, which represents family and friends—those closest to us. Then it overflows into the third bowl of community and country. Finally, it overflows into the fourth bowl, which represents the world! Jesus told his disciples to go to Jerusalem and wait until they had received the Holy Spirit. Then he said to them—Acts 1:8, my paraphrase—now, go and [overflow] in Jerusalem, and then go on and [overflow] in Judea, and [overflow] in Samaria, and to the ends of the earth!

But, first things first; it had to begin with the disciples, and today, it must begin with you and me. Our relationship with God and how much we allow the Holy Spirit to fill us will determine whether or not we overflow at all. Now, let's ask the tough question: Are you an overflowing fountain? Or, are you a clogged up fountain? A barely trickling fountain? Or a dried up fountain?

What happens when the first bowl begins to restrict the water flow? It affects the other bowls! What happens when the first bowl decides, "it's all about me!" and wants to hoard all the blessings for "me?" What that says is, "I don't care about my family and friends, I don't care about the people in this community, and I don't care about the world I only care about me! Serve me, love me, teach me, bless me, and listen to me! Let everyone else worry about themselves. I will only get involved if it serves my purpose. It's all about *me me me!*

If the early church in the book of Acts worked that way, we wouldn't be here today. If we don't flow we won't grow, and we will soon become stagnant and dry up. As I drive by that motel on Highway 29, I have a vision of a beautiful fountain. One that can be seen for a mile in both directions; brightly lit up at night;

sitting in the middle of an oasis of beautiful trees and landscaping. It's an attractive setting that says, "Come to me, all you who are weary, and burdened, and I will give you rest" (Matthew 11:28). Maybe we should put a fountain like that in front of every church!

Let me pass on a story from the book *Outflow*, by Steve Sjogren and Dave Ping, about a man named Pastor John:

> John is a pastor who'd been sent all the way from a remote part of Kenya to complete training in Ohio. Soon after he arrived in Ohio, he got a call from his brother back home in Kenya. From the look on John's face, it was clear that he'd received some terrible news. He relayed to his wife Pam; "Bandits have come in the night and taken my family's milk cow.
>
> It may not sound like a big deal to you. However, in the famine stricken area of Kenya where John was from, that one cow was all that stood between John's family, the eleven orphans he had adopted, and certain starvation. By the time he finished talking, Pam knew she had to do something right away. Minutes later, normally frugal Pam, was in her car on the way to the Western Union office to wire John's family enough money to buy a top quality milk cow. Meanwhile, within ten minutes of letting the other conference attendees know of his need, John had more than enough money to buy three cows.
>
> Though John felt certain God wanted him to come to America to this training, he was deeply concerned for his family and his little village

ever since he left. Overwhelmed by the immediate and generous response from people he'd never met, John tearfully reflected; "If I had been home, I would have fought those bandits and I probably would have been killed. God is so good. I trusted him enough to come here and he has saved both me and my family!"

John didn't use the money to buy three more cows. No, he gave away all the rest to teachers in his village school that hadn't been paid in over a year! "God has blessed me" he said, "How could I do any less for them?"[23] Blessed to be a blessing.

"Do you still not see or understand? Are your hearts hardened? Do you have eyes but fail to see, and ears but fail to hear?"

Mark 8:18

"Though seeing, they do not see; though hearing, they do not hear or understand. In them is fulfilled the prophecy of Isaiah: "You will be ever hearing but never understanding; you will be ever seeing but never perceiving. For this people's heart has become calloused; they hardly hear with their ears, and they have closed their eyes. Otherwise they might see with their eyes, hear with their ears, understand with their hearts and turn, and I would heal them. But blessed are your eyes because they see, and your ears because they hear."

Matthew 13:13–16

> "I keep asking that the God of our Lord Jesus Christ, the glorious Father, may give you the Spirit of wisdom and revelation, so that you may know him better. I pray also that the eyes of your heart may be enlightened in order that you may know the hope to which He has called you, the riches of his glorious inheritance in the saints, and His incomparably great power for us who believe."
>
> Ephesians 1:18–19

The reason I put these scriptures together is to show that a person cannot *overflow;* in fact they cannot even be filled, unless they have "eyes (spiritual) that can see" and "ears (spiritual) that can hear" what the Spirit of wisdom and revelation is saying and teaching them. I believe that when a person comes to Christ and accepts the free gift of God's grace and forgiveness through Christ and Christ alone, that person is not only saved from eternal death and the lake of fire; but that person is also *given, marked, sealed,* and *filled* with as much of the Holy Spirit of God as they are going to get. Let me explain that.

In the book of Ephesians 1:13, it says this:

> "And you also were included in Christ when you *heard the word of truth,* the *gospel* of your salvation. *Having believed,* you were *marked* in him with a *seal,* the promised Holy Spirit, who is a deposit guaranteeing our inheritance until the redemption of those who are God's possession—to the praise of his glory."

These things are all past tense! You heard and believed, were marked and were sealed! Then Paul goes on to say:

> "I keep asking that the God of our Lord Jesus Christ, the glorious Father, may give you the Spirit of wisdom and revelation, so that you may know him better. I pray also that the *eyes of your heart may be enlightened* in order that you may know"—three things—"the *hope* to which He has called you" [past tense, we already have it.] "the *riches* of His glorious inheritance in the saints" ("inheritance" is a future word.) and His incomparably *great power* for us who believe." (present tense, it's available now!)

When he says, "I pray that God will give you the Spirit of wisdom and revelation," that is something you can only get when you come to Christ through the gospel of salvation. This is also why Paul tells us that "the things of the Spirit are foolishness to those who are without the Spirit"!

What that says to me is that when we ask and allow the Holy Spirit to open our spiritual eyes and ears; when we really "hunger and thirst after righteousness" as his Word says; and we become uninhibited in our worship and consistent in our "seeking"; we will begin to know and believe and understand that God is who he says he is, and God can do what he says he can do, and I am who God says I am not who the world or my parents or my so called friends or even my enemies say I am and that I can do all things through Christ Jesus! Therefore, nothing is impossible, and, in fact, all things are possible with God! When I truly and assuredly and absolutely believe that, then and only then will all this begin to overflow from me and spill over into my family and friends, into my community, and yes, even into our world!

This is what happened to the disciples, and it says that they turned the world upside down! *It can't flow from you unless it is in you!* Is the Spirit of God flowing? Are we allowing the Spirit to flow? Or are we stifling the Spirit of God? Is anybody around us getting wet? Or are we as dry as the bones that lay before Ezekiel? If we are, then we need God to breathe new life into our parched souls and bring forth the life-giving water of the Spirit once again! Amen?

Maybe we need to go back and find our first love. In the book of Revelation, the second chapter, Jesus tells the church at Ephesus that they have "lost their first love," and he says "repent and do the things you did at first." What started your church? What did the first people do that established and grew your church in the beginning? From the historical records, I know that in my church in Altavista, Virginia, there was a revival in a place called Rabbit Hollow and a handful of folks, who were saved and seeking, started a fellowship and a Bible study, and they began to overflow in their hunger for God and their desire to build a church. Why? What was their purpose? What was their first love? I believe it was a burning desire for their families, friends, and others in the community—and yes, even the world—to know what they had come to know! The love, joy, peace, forgiveness, and transforming power of God to change lives!

Let me quickly give you just two factors that I have experienced that have caused even me to lose focus, to lose sight of my first love. Both are tactics of the enemy to steal our time and energy from God.

The first is the hurry factor. Go here, go there, do this, do that; the "to do" list keeps growing, and it seems we have less and less time or energy to keep up. In fact, our favorite and most often used excuses are "I don't have time" or "I just don't feel like it." Satan has gotten even me to use those at times when it comes to my own ministry! Or how about "I'm not interested in what is being taught," "that doesn't really apply to me," or "I have better things to do!" Listen, these are not excuses; they are lies! They are lies that Satan uses to keep us away from God and hinder us from doing his work. Let me ask a point blank question; "Do you go to Worship on Sunday to hear the preacher talk or to hear God speak? If your answer is honestly "to hear God speak," then what about Sunday school, Sunday night, or Wednesday night? God is there; where are you?

The second is the worry factor: "What am I going to do?" "How am I going to make it?" "How will I pay those bills?" "What if… ?" If Satan can get us to fall into the worry factor, he can get us to try and take control of our own lives and think that if we let go, everything will fall apart. He will try to convince us that, if I'm going to make it, it's up to me!

Worry is a lack of trust that God's way is the best way. Worry is a lack of trust that God knows me well enough to know my every need and that he will supply that need. I preach about it and yet fall into Satan's worry trap myself! I think this is the kind of thing Paul is talking about when he says, "I do what I don't want to do, and what I should do, I don't do" and o-da-doo-da-day (my paraphrase of Romans 7:14–21).

I have fallen prey to these two factors that cause us to take our eyes off of God, and I have gotten a wake up call. And it has become my prayer and my desire that each one of us who is willing, would ask God to fill us to overflowing with his Word, his Spirit, his love, and his joy, so we would begin to live life from the overflow! Water that does not flow soon becomes stagnant. We don't want to even talk about what happens in and around stagnant water.

It begins within each one of us. We must first have the Holy Spirit in us; that's the first step. If you have accepted God's work of grace through Jesus Christ his Son, if you have sought forgiveness and asked him to come in to your heart and life, he has! His Holy Spirit is there, waiting for your commitment and waiting to receive more and more of you until he overflows!

The more we open ourselves up to God, seek after righteousness, and hunger for his Word and come with a teachable spirit, the more he will "pour into our lives and fill us," and as Paul prays, the more "the eyes of our hearts will be enlightened." The more we give, the more we get! And, finally, we must allow the Holy Spirit to overflow from us, into our families, our friends, our coworkers, our community, and into the world. Amen?

Next, we will focus on the second bowl of this spiritual fountain, and how we can overflow into the lives of family and friends.

Part 2:

OVERFLOWING TO THOSE CLOSEST TO US

"Now he who supplies *seed* to the sower and bread for food will also supply and increase your store of *seed* and will enlarge the harvest of your righteousness. You will be made rich in every way so that you can be generous on every occasion, and through us your generosity will result in thanksgiving to God.

This service that you perform is not only supplying the needs of God's people but is also overflowing in many expressions of thanks to God. Because of the service by which you have proved yourselves, men will praise God for the obedience that accompanies your confession of the gospel of Christ, and for your generosity in sharing with them and with everyone else. And in their prayers for you their hearts will go out to you, because of the surpassing grace God has given you. Thanks be to God for his indescribable gift!"

2 Corinthians 9:10–13

First, we turned our focus on the first tier of the fountain—ourselves, showing how we must allow the Holy Spirit to flow into us and to fill us. Then and only then, can the Spirit work through us and overflow from us as we pour out and use his blessings to us. Those blessings come in many ways physically, emotionally, and spiritually. Even the fruit of the Spirit, which is love, joy, peace, patience, goodness, kindness, and self-control, that is in us, can overflow from us!

Let's turn our focus to this second tier of the fountain.

There are three ways that we can overflow into our families, our community, and even the world. Jesus used three different analogies or word pictures to get this point across. We have probably heard them several times, but maybe not from this perspective of the Holy Spirit working through us and overflowing from us. First, Jesus said we were to be "salt." Second, he said we were to be "light." And here in this scripture, we are to be what I would call "seed casters."

Although I didn't use the Parable of the Sower from Matthew 13 as my text, I have included part of it so you can read it once again, and then I will comment on the parts that apply.

Jesus said that a man "went out to sow his seed." Some fell along the path, some fell on rocky, shallow soil, some fell among thorns, and some fell on good soil, where it produced a good crop.

:

> "Listen then to what the parable of the sower means: When anyone hears the message about the kingdom and does not understand it, the evil

> one comes and snatches away what was sown in his heart. This is the seed sown along the path. The one who received the seed that fell on rocky places is the man who hears the word and at once receives it with joy. But since he has no root, he lasts only a short time. When trouble or persecution comes because of the word, he quickly falls away. The one who received the seed that fell among the thorns is the man who hears the word, but the worries of this life and the deceitfulness of wealth choke it, making it unfruitful. But the one who received the seed that fell on good soil is the man who hears the word and understands it. He produces a crop, yielding a hundred, sixty or thirty times what was sown."
>
> Matthew 13:18–23

Part of allowing the Holy Spirit to overflow from us involves us being "sowers" casting seeds. However, we need to know that when it comes to our families and our friends, and our coworkers and neighbors, they are all in very different places spiritually. Their heart may be like a path, and they feel like they have been walked on and beaten down. It may be even hard and rocky, because of some experience that has somehow turned them off to the church. It could be that the thorns, the weeds, and the worries of this life have them feeling like life is passing them by or like something is choking the life out of them. Not everyone is ready or willing to hear that Jesus loves them and died for them!

It's not our Bible knowledge or our "fear of hell" techniques that they are interested in. It's our tangible and visible expressions of what we believe. They are what I call *seeds of action,* which contain God's love working through us.

Again, from 1 Corinthians 13,

> "If I speak in the tongues of men and of angels, but have not love, I am only a resounding gong or a clanging cymbal. If I have the gift of prophecy and can fathom all mysteries and all knowledge, and if I have a faith that can move mountains, but have not love, I am nothing. If I give all I possess to the poor and surrender my body to the flames, but have not love, I gain nothing."

So we must always sow seeds of God's love remembering that the soil is always different. We must also remember that just a couple of verses previous—in 2 Corinthians 9:6—it tells us that where there is little seed sown, there is little harvest: "Remember this: Whoever sows sparingly will also reap sparingly, and whoever sows generously will also reap generously." If we are not seeing any harvest, maybe we ought to check how—or how much—we are casting seed!

One research team was sent on the streets to ask what people thought of Christians who evangelize? Unfortunately, the most frequent comments were: "annoying," "pushy," "rude," "arrogant," "disrespectful," and "turn offs!" In other words, negative experiences! Isn't it something that what is supposed to be "good news" is "bad news" to many people? That, my friends, is bad news; not only to the recipients, but also to the messengers! Let me ask this. How do you feel when the Jehovah's Witness come to your door? Many people see all Christians as they view the Jehovah's Witnesses! I don't know about you, but that doesn't get me really excited about scattering seeds!

But, remember, there are many styles of evangelism, and even though we can't always tell by looking at the outside what kind of soil is on the inside, there are some seeds we can and must plant no matter what the soil may be. I will list them as (1) listening seeds, (2) kindness seeds, and (3) sharing seeds.

Someone once said, "In a world where talk is cheap, good listening is pure gold." Quite often, when it comes to our families and friends, using our ears more and our mouth less is far more effective. James 1:19 says, "Everyone should be quick to listen, slow to speak and slow to become angry." At times when we are tempted to respond or react in a conversation, we need to zip it and just listen. We need to watch body language and pay attention to feelings. This sends a signal that we value the person and their needs and that we genuinely want to help, pray, and stand by them.

Romans 12:15 tells us to, "Rejoice with those who rejoice; mourn with those who mourn." When it comes to our families and friends, we often have an overwhelming need to disagree or correct beliefs or behaviors that we think are unacceptable. But James tells us we ought to be "quick to listen and slow to speak" or slow to "put our two cents in!" It's the best way to sow *listening seeds.* It becomes much more effective to say, "How can I help" rather than "Let me tell you what you should do!"

Second, we can overflow into the lives of our

friends and family when we sow *seeds of kindness.* Acts of kindness that are not solicited, but things we do just, because we care and Jesus cares. James 2:14–16 asks us to consider; "What good is it, my brothers, if a man claims to have faith but has no deeds? Can such faith save him? Suppose a brother or sister is without clothes and daily food. If one of you says to him, "Go, I wish you well; keep warm and well fed," but does nothing about his physical needs, what good is it? In the same way, faith by itself, if it is not accompanied by action, is dead."

Physical needs are just one way we can sow seeds of kindness, but there are literally thousands of ways that are not necessarily physical needs. In fact, I heard of a group that was started of those interested in a *kindness* ministry. They just think about and do things that are just random acts of kindness. We need a group like this in every church!

The third thing we can do is cast *seeds of sharing.* While this may sound like sharing material and monetary blessings, which is good, it has more to do with sharing our faith, beliefs, and experiences, as we witness and give testimony. This is about making sure we let our families and friends know about the things that God does in our lives. Sharing those times—those *kiros* moments—when we experience God. I am thinking not only personal experiences, but also, when you experience the hand of God blessing your church as well.

In one story of Jesus healing the blind man, the Pharisees questioned him as to who Jesus was and what had really happened. He simply said, "All I know is I was blind, and now I see!" We don't have to have some *philosophical, theological, and ideological* explanation of all that God does; we just have to share our experiences.

Mother Teresa once said, "It is not the magnitude of our actions, but the amount of love we put into them that matters." If you think this business of pouring or flowing into the lives of others is not that important, consider the survey that shows that less than five out of one hundred people indicated they came to faith in Christ through some evangelistic means like crusades, revivals, TV preachers, or Bible tracts. But more than ninety-five percent said it was because of their relationship with someone close to them who demonstrated their faith in the tangible ways you have just read about. It is through listening, and casting seeds of kindness, and sharing our faith whenever appropriate, we pour into others in ways that show God's love and blessing.

Listen once again to the words of 2 Corinthians 9:10,

> "Now he who supplies seed to the sower and bread for food will also supply and *increase* your store of seed and will *enlarge* the harvest of your righteousness ... This service that you perform is not only supplying the needs of God's people but is also *overflowing* in many expressions of thanks to God. Because of the service by which you have proved yourselves, men will praise God for the obedience that accompanies your confession of the gospel of Christ and for your generosity in sharing with them and with everyone else."

Are you getting the picture?

If we look for ways to pour into the lives of those in tier number two of our fountain—those closest to us—God will pour into us so we will have all that we need and will never run out of seed to sow. Look at what Paul calls this "surpassing grace" of listening, kindness, and sharing; he calls it an "indescribable gift!" It brings a blessing so great, you can't describe it!

Part 3:

OVERFLOWING TO THE COMMUNITY

"Jesus answered, "Everyone who drinks this water will be thirsty again, but whoever drinks the water I give him will never thirst. Indeed, the water I give him will become in him a spring of water welling up to eternal life."

John 4:13–14

"On the last and greatest day of the Feast, Jesus stood and said in a loud voice, "If anyone is thirsty, let him come to me and drink. Whoever believes in me, as the Scripture has said, streams of living water will flow from within him." By this He meant the Spirit, whom those who believed in him were later to receive."

John 7:37–38

> "O Jerusalem, Jerusalem, you who kill the prophets and stone those sent to you, how often I have longed to gather your children together, as a hen gathers her chicks under her wings, but you were not willing."
>
> Matthew 23:37

It always begins with us. Unless we have come to Christ and have a relationship with God through the indwelling Holy Spirit, we do not have anything to give, nothing to fill us; and therefore, we are like a dried up fountain. Our life, and even the life of our church will reflect that. But, Jesus says; "Whoever believes in me, as the Scripture has said, steams of living water will flow from within him. Indeed, the water I give him will become a spring of water welling up to eternal life!" This is the basis as we look at the third tier of the fountain, which is pouring out, or overflowing, into our community.

One thing we can discover about Jesus is that he liked to simplify things. Consider for instance the fact that the religious leaders, the Sadducees, the Pharisees, the Herodians, and the Zealots, had developed a religious system with six hundred and thirteen laws. In their opinion, there were six hundred and thirteen commandments in the Pentateuch, the first five books of the Bible. They divided those laws into affirmative commands (do this) and negative commands (don't do that). There ended up being two hundred and forty-eight affirmative commands and three hundred and sixty-five negative commands (one for each day of the year.) They further divided these into binding and non-binding commands and spent their days debating the accuracy and ranking of the commands within the division ... Whew! Enter Jesus.

The story is found in Matthew 22. Jesus has just stumped the Sadducees, and next up were the Pharisees. They gather for a quick meeting, they choose the smartest guy—a lawyer—and he asks Jesus, "Which is the greatest commandment in the law?" In other words, of all the six hundred and thirteen commandments, which is the greatest, the most important? Jesus simply says, "Love the Lord your God with all your heart mind and soul, and love your neighbor as yourself." Now, listen to what he says here: "*All* the law and the Prophets depend on these two commandments!" Think about the true significance of that simple statement. Everything about the Christian life is going to be dependent on those two things!

Unless we (1) love the Lord our God and unless we (2) love our neighbor, we will not be motivated to make any kind of significant difference in the church, much less the lives of our families, our community, or our world. In fact, John tells us in the book of 1 John, that we can't say we love our neighbor unless we love God! Unless we truly love God, we won't read his Word, we won't attend church, we won't evangelize, we won't reach out, we won't get involved, and we will be nothing more than a bunch of "clanging cymbals" who gather in a holy huddle on Sunday mornings!

But, if we love God like we say we do, then his love will flow through us and overflow from us into the lives of our families and friends, into our community, and on into the world! We ought to ask ourselves this simple question: "What is it about me, which shows my family and friends, and to the people in my community, and to the world for that matter, that I am a Christian?"

"Well, I dress up and go to church on Sundays, so, surely they know that I am a Christian!"

"Well, I read my Bible and a daily devotional every day!"

"Well, I not only do all that, but I also serve on the church board and several other committees!"

While that's all wonderful stuff, God's Word says that they will know we are Christians by our *love;* Our love for one another and for others that is demonstrated in tangible and visible ways.

Consider what Jesus is saying in the last scripture of our text. Consider the cry of his heart when he looks out over Jerusalem and says "How I have longed to gather your children together as a hen gathers her chicks under her wings." Words like *love, safety, protection, healing, comfort,* and *salvation* come to mind. He longed for their salvation, because of their sin, their stubbornness, their suffering, and because of their separation from God. So, how do you see your community? I am here to tell you, they are just like the people of Jerusalem! In order for us to make a difference at all, we must look out over the people of our community with the same longing and loving desire that Jesus had for Jerusalem!

I said previously that when people were asked their opinions of Christians, most had negative things to say. But I also believe that the only thing that can change anyone's perspective is for people to personally experience Christ's love for them first hand. Perhaps that's why Jesus said the two greatest commandments are both about love. I'm not talking about preaching to them or handing out tracts or even starting a homeless shelter—those are different. I'm talking about what would happen if we loved God so much that we would let what he feels for the people in our community begin to overflow into our own hearts. What if every time we looked at the people of our community and the people around us, we literally longed for them to know Jesus, even if they have purple hair and tattoos and rings in their lips? What if we longed for God to gather them in his arms and show them his love for them—through us? What if it were just "normal" for us to intentionally pour out kind words, actions, and scatter seeds of kindness? What kind of a difference would that make?

In the book "Outflow" the author puts it this way; "What if you intentionally set out to do some small act of kindness for one person every day? Every week you would touch seven individuals. If you did this every week for a year, that would be about 365 acts of kindness in Jesus name. And that's just one person!"[24] Now, multiply that by, say, fifty people, which is the average size of a small church, and you get 18,250 small acts of kindness in one year. I'm not talking about some program that would be nice to try. I'm talking about an overflowing lifestyle!

Two things will happen: the person you say you are and the person others see when they meet you will become a little more Christlike, and their perspective of Christians and the church just might change.

I'm not talking about big things, just small acts of kindness. Buy someone lunch (even someone you don't know), let someone in front of you in line, hold the door, offer to help mow the neighbor's yard—the list of opportunities is endless. These little drops of love will fall into all kinds of soil, some may even land in a heart ready to seek Jesus. The "frosting on the cake," so to speak, would be taking opportunities to share this overflowing life and the inspiring true experiences that we have with God and have someone get saved!

Not long ago, on Sunday evenings in one of my churches, we went through a series called *Better Together* by Rick Warren. It was all about how we can accomplish so much more in ministry and life when we work together. One of the things that was suggested that we do, is just what I'm talking about—acts of kindness. We were going to come together to help with projects around the house for widows and the elderly in our community. Many churches push this off on the youth group, but what if we all got involved?

Let me paint another "overflowing" picture in your minds eye; each one of us is like a drop of rain. The more it rains, the more water that flows. The water flows into the ditches and creeks, which then flow into the rivers and streams, many of which eventually find their way to the ocean. Jesus didn't just call us to be raindrops, he called us to go and fill the ocean! It takes a lot of drops flowing together to fill the ocean.

Let me close this part with this, and we must understand this thought: It's not about my church or your church; it's about *the* church. It's about bringing people into the kingdom. It's about knowing that God is who he says he is, and that God can do what he says he can do! However, he needs willing and open vessels ready for the overflowing, life-giving, life-transforming, and fountain-filling water of the Holy Spirit!

In the book of Acts, chapter two, on the Day of Pentecost, Peter stood and quoted the Prophet Joel in saying,

> "In the last days, I will pour out my Spirit on all people. Your sons and daughters will prophecy, your young men will see visions, and your old men will dream dreams. Even on my servants both men and women, I will pour out my Spirit in those days ... And, everyone who calls upon the name of the Lord will be saved!"

I believe we are living in those "last days," and we best be about the Lord's business! Amen.

John Wesley said, "Do all the good you can, by all the means you can, in all the ways you can, in all the places you can, at all the times you can, to all the people you can, as long as ever you can."

Steve Sjogren, who wrote *Conspiracy of Kindness* said,

> "For most Christians, doing evangelism is a lot like going to the dentist; no one really enjoys doing it, but it must done once in a while. But anyone can do simple acts of kindness. People don't necessarily remember what they are *told* of God's love, but they never forget what they have *experienced* of God's love."[25]

Evangelism is a team effort. By showing folks the love of God, we can create an interest in them that may cause them to want to know more about the God who moves us to act with kindness. Every AOK (Act Of Kindness) we do, is like sowing a seed. We just plant the seed, and God will make it grow!

Part 4:

OVERFLOWING TO THE WORLD

"He said to them, "This is what I told you while I was still with you: Everything must be fulfilled that is written about me in the Law of Moses, the Prophets and the Psalms." Then He opened their minds so they could understand the Scriptures. He told them, "This is what is written: The Christ will suffer and rise from the dead on the third day, and repentance and forgiveness of sins will be preached in His name to all nations, beginning at Jerusalem. You are witnesses of these things. I am going to send you what my Father has promised; but stay in the city until you have been clothed with power from on high. When He had led them out to the vicinity of Bethany, He lifted up his hands and blessed them. While He was blessing them, He left them and was taken up into heaven. Then they worshiped Him and returned to Jerusalem with great joy. And they stayed continually at the temple, praising God."

Luke 24:44–53

"In my former book, Theophilus, I wrote about all that Jesus began to do and to teach until the day he was taken up to heaven, after giving instructions through the Holy Spirit to the apostles he had chosen. After His suffering, He showed himself to these men and gave many convincing proofs that He was alive. He appeared to them over a period of forty days and spoke about the kingdom of God. On one occasion, while He was eating with them, He gave them this command: "Do not leave Jerusalem, but wait for the gift my Father promised, which you have heard me speak about. For John baptized with water, but in a few days you will be baptized with the Holy Spirit." So when they met together, they asked Him, "Lord, are you at this time going to restore the kingdom to Israel?" He said to them: "It is not for you to know the times or dates the Father has set by his own authority. But you will receive power when the Holy Spirit comes on you; and you will be my witnesses in Jerusalem, and in all Judea and Samaria, and to the ends of the earth."

Acts 1:1–8

"Then Jesus came to them and said, "All authority in heaven and on earth has been given to me. Therefore go and make disciples of all nations, baptizing them in the name of the Father and of the Son and of the Holy Spirit, and teaching them to obey everything I have commanded you. And surely I am with you always, to the very end of the age."

Matthew 28:18–20

Have you ever been a part of a scene like this?

"What do you want to do?"

"I don't know what do you want to do?"

"I don't know what to you want to do?"

"Well, what do you think we should do?"

"I don't know."

"Me either!"

Do you know that this is one of the pictures I have in my mind when it comes to the church? Yet, when you think about it, this should never be the case in the church because we have been given the instruction manual! Because of God's Word and because of who Jesus is, what a Christian is to do is already determined for us. Therefore, there should be no need for Christians to get together in the church and ask each other, "What do you want to?"

"I don't know, what to you think we should do?"

Jesus' final instructions before leaving planet Earth were go, witness, make disciples, baptize, and teach in Jerusalem, Judea, Samaria, and to the ends of the earth. Basically, that covers about every area of influence we can have!

There are other scriptures of course, that tell us that we are *ambassadors* for Christ, and we are to carry the *good news* of the gospel to all nations. Another scripture calls this the ministry of reconciliation. The problem is that we as Christians, and as part of the church, have wasted all our time and energy on two things:

1. Trying to decide what to do: "What do you want to do?" And, if we do make a

decision on what to do, we get stuck on number two.

2. "How should we do it?"

If you are thinking I have the answer to those two questions, I don't. Not specifically anyway. But, God does. I do know this: God has already told us *what* we ought to be doing, and he has also shown us *how* it must be done through the enabling power of the Holy Spirit flowing in and through us. Influencing first, those around us and closest to us, then overflowing and influencing our community, and finally, overflowing, influencing, and affecting our world. That has always been God's plan. However, it begins with us! We need to seek the *how* through prayer.

There are three major factors that will determine if we ever get anything accomplished for God:

1. We must see the need.
2. We must catch the vision of how God can and does fill the need.
3. We must be willing vessels.

If any one of those three factors is missing, God cannot accomplish anything through us, or the church. We can see the need. And, we can also see how God fills the need in many different ways. But, if you look again at those three factors, I think you would agree that number three, be willing vessels, is usually the problem.

Conclusion:

FOUR REASONS WHY THIS IS IMPORTANT NOW

There are four reasons why all of this is so important to us as Christians today. The first is because of the size of the task. There are over six billion people on this planet, and the population is ever increasing. Some view that with a negative vision. "How can we possibly accomplish the task?" Well, how do you eat an elephant? One bite at a time. Others view the task with a positive attitude like that of John Wesley's: "Let's reach as many as we can, in as many ways as we can, with all that we can, in as many places as we can, as long as we can!"

The second reason this is so important is because of the need. We all know the basic needs are food, shelter, medicine, and education, and we have to do all that we can to help provide those basic needs both at home and abroad. But there is a need that is deeper still; that is the profound emptiness of the heart and soul. It's not enough to give bread to eat; we also must provide the bread of life, Jesus Christ, who is the only way to eternal life!

The third reason we must catch God's vision for the world and be willing vessels is because of the competition we face. Islam, which is growing in numbers in America, uses all the same technologies to reach people that we use. Buddhism has hundreds of missionaries in America. They even have preaching services and Sunday school programs. Hinduism, whose chief message is "tolerance," considers America its greatest mission field. What about the Mormons or the Jehovah's Witnesses, the Moonies, the New Age movement, and Secular Humanism? But the church's greatest enemy has always been Satan himself, and his greatest weapon is apathy!

Yes, we are facing the biggest task, the deepest need, and strong competition, but listen, we still have the fourth reason: it's because we have the greatest message the world has ever heard and still needs to hear! We must catch God's vision for the world and become willing vessels!

It is the only message that can turn darkness to light, despair into hope, and physical, mental, emotional and spiritual bondage into freedom! It can turn death into life, proclaim forgiveness for sin, and transform lives! It's the message, "you shall know the truth, and the truth will set you free!" Buddha is dead! Mohammed is dead! Jesus is alive! The world needs to hear it!

I am excited about this part of being an *overflowing* Christian, because not only do we have the greatest message to give to the world, we also have the greatest power in us and ahead of us the world has ever known! I say *ahead* of us, because all other faiths are *manmade* and ours is *Spirit-led!* It is "Spirit-filled!" And, it is supposed to be overflowing!

My final question is this: "What do you want to do?"

When Jesus was twelve years old, he went to Jerusalem with Joseph and his mother. When his parents were returning home, they could not find Jesus. Like any concerned parents, they went looking for him and found him in the temple listening to and talking with the teachers. When Mary spoke of their concern, Jesus responded, "Didn't you know that I had to be about my Father's business?"

There are three ways we all can be involved in the Father's business: We can go, we can give, and we can pray. We can also be a part of all three! Why? Because Jesus said, "When you have been clothed with power from on high … when the Holy Spirit comes upon you … you will be my witnesses in Jerusalem, [to your family and friends] in Judea and Samaria [to your community and surrounding area], and to the ends of the earth!"

When Jesus ascended into heaven, and the disciples watched him disappear, it says that they stood there, "gazing into the sky." Then two angels appeared and said (my paraphrase), "What are you waiting for? Jesus is coming back … and we best be about the Father's business!"

To that I say–Amen!

Endnotes

Chapter 1

1 Taken from *JohnThree: Sixteen* by R.L. Moyer onlinebaptist.com devotional for Nov. 7th.

2 Hymn by F.M. Lehman published 1938 Sword of the Lord

3 Author unknown

4 Unknown

5 Unknown

6 Originated as a short story written by Dennis E. Hensley first published in Michigan Baptist Bulletin in 1967

7 Unknown

8 Internet - unknown

9 Unknown

10 Hymn "Whosoever Will" Words and Music by Philip P. Bliss, 1870

Chapter 2

11 Used by permission. Excerpts taken from *Believing God.* Beth Moore. ©2004 B&H Publishing Group

12 Used by permission. Excerpts taken from *Believing God.* Beth Moore. ©2004 B&H Publishing Group

13 Unknown

14 Based on rumor. Alan Smith. *Heartlight,* Abilene, TX

15 Used by permission. Excerpts taken from *Believing God.* Beth Moore. ©2004 B&H Publishing Group

Chapter 3

16 *Knowing God.* Intervarsity Press.

17 *York Station View.* Knowing God Through the Year devotional.

18 Unknown source

19 Unknown source

20 Unknown source

Chapter 5

21 *Loving Across Our Differences.* Gerald Sittser. Intervarsity Press

Chapter 6

22 *Natural Church Development.* Christian A. Schwarz. Church Smart Resources

23 *Outflow* by Steve Sjogren and Dave Ping. Group Publishing

Chapter 7

24 *Outflow* by Steve Sjogren and Dave Ping. Group Publishing

25 *Conspiracy of Kindness* Steve Sjogren. Regal Books

e|LIVE

listen|imagine|view|experience

AUDIO BOOK DOWNLOAD INCLUDED WITH THIS BOOK!

In your hands you hold a complete digital entertainment package. Besides purchasing the paper version of this book, this book includes a free download of the audio version of this book. Simply use the code listed below when visiting our website. Once downloaded to your computer, you can listen to the book through your computer's speakers, burn it to an audio CD or save the file to your portable music device (such as Apple's popular iPod) and listen on the go!

How to get your free audio book digital download:

1. Visit www.tatepublishing.com and click on the e|LIVE logo on the home page.
2. Enter the following coupon code: bf63-776d-5a44-6ffe-44d4-ceef-2791-e8a2
3. Download the audio book from your e|LIVE digital locker and begin enjoying your new digital entertainment package today!